The Hawthorn Tree

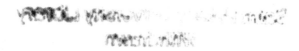

THE HAWTHORN TREE

Some Papers and Letters on Life and the Theatre

BY

PAUL GREEN

Essay Index Reprint Series

BOOKS FOR LIBRARIES PRESS
FREEPORT, NEW YORK

INTERNATIONAL STANDARD BOOK NUMBER:

0-8369-2228-X

LIBRARY OF CONGRESS CATALOG CARD NUMBER:

79-134085

PRINTED IN THE UNITED STATES OF AMERICA

FOR THE THREE SISTERS
GLADYS, CARO MAE, ERMA

A few of these articles have appeared in earlier form in *The Carolina Playbook, The National Theatre Conference Bulletin, The New York Times, Theatre Arts Magazine* and as prefaces. Acknowledgments and thanks are herewith made for the right to reprint.

He cropped off the top of his young twigs, and carried it into a land of traffick; he set it in a city of merchants. He took also of the seed of the land, and planted it in a fruitful field . . . and it grew.

Ezekiel 17: 4-5.

"And if unto the dead thou art fain to do good, or if thou wouldst work them ill—'tis all one, since they feel not joy or grief. Nevertheless our righteous resentment is mightier than they, and Justice executeth the dead man's wrath." Aeschylus.

Contents

The Hawthorn Tree

Preface for Professors

1

IN THIS PRESENT TRAGIC YEAR SOME SEVERAL HUNDRED
thousand of our young American men and women, repre-
senting an original class more than a million strong, are
graduating from our colleges and universities and setting
forth down the long road that leads up over the horizon
and beyond. There somewhere, they are told, wait the
remainder of the life they are to live and the fruits that
life will bear. There wait the joys, the heartaches, the
successes and failure that will be their lot. It is for that
life ahead that they have spent these years of preparation
—of instruction and dedicated study. It is for this their
parents have sacrificed, friends and the taxpayers con-
tributed their money, and the teachers their devoted
effort and encouragement.

When they came to our campuses some four years ago
they were eager and happy boys and girls no doubt, and
the world was a beautiful and inspiring place to live in.

They were sharp and sensitive as the morning air they breathed. And it was not all carrots and vitamin B bouncing in their veins. It was the tingling spirits of a life in the growing, swelling with expectancy, idealism, and wonder. Before them was the bright rainbow of hope and the promise of things to be fulfilled, and their hearts leapt up to see that promise in the sky. They thrilled to feel the glad new days come rushing on, they were anxious to get at the business of learning something new, something that would give them a wider reach, a broader view, a clearer comprehension of themselves and their fellow man. So much an education must mean to them.

And everywhere around them stood the proofs and tokens of the glorious enterprise on which they had embarked. They were filled with admiration, even awe, before our great buildings, our laboratories, chapels, bell towers, stadiums, and vast libraries. And in their wondering eyes we professors ourselves seemed to them much more than ordinary men. For were we not the high priests of the grey-eyed goddess truth, and were we not possessed of deep knowledge and the lore of the ancients, sacred and profane? And did not our vision go far beyond that of their own fathers who perhaps built roads, ran trains, farmed, sold insurance, worked in a powerhouse, or talked over the radio about the grace of God and chewing gum?

2

So it was that they were matriculated, as we call it, and were college students at last. Then their training began and it began in a hurry. For four years would be gone all too swiftly and in that short time they must be moulded into the well-rounded citizen, the upstanding and dynamic individual ready for all emergencies. So without more ado than to give them time for a couple of soft drinks and a short cheap gangster movie maybe, we learned men set out to initiate them with all the methodology and techniques at our command. We first looked at them, walked round them, peered into their eyes and measured them. With instruments and strange devices we tested their mentality. And with queer and tricky riddles, with little signs and symbols which might damn them forever for all they knew, we hunted for their aptitude. Words and pictures, blocks and mazes we tried them with, watching their reaction, how swift, how slow, and how far above or below a mystic concept known as the norm they might prove to be. And when we'd got a threatening bead drawn clean upon their naked soul, the history of their cases all written down, we carried off their pure IQ and locked it up. And they were classified.

Their courses were then laid out, their subjects marked and approved. And like the pilgrim in the fable they were supposed to reach these subjects one by one and to gather succor and strength from each dwelling place as they progressed. And when finally they would land on the shore of graduation day they would be strong, well-trained, and ready to mix joyfully and surely in the game of life being played there upon the sands of time close by the breakers' beat—so the commencement speakers said to them.

In spite of this puzzling ritual of initiation they went obediently and trustfully to work. They took as they were told their curriculum in language and literature, the sciences, mathematics, and in the various other fields.

And whatever we prescribed they in the main tried to carry out. For this was being in college now, this was preparing one's self for life. So they studied hard and believed the things we told them and the sacred textbooks they read, and walked in wonder and the burden of learning cloaking round them. For a while they did.

Then strangely enough as the days went by a change began to happen in them. In their sophomore year we noticed it—those of us not shut away writing for learned journals did. And by their junior year it was even more pronounced. They had become a little suspicious and even distrustful of their former prophets of truth. By their senior year it was pretty obvious—they felt we were more to be listened to than followed. The real he-men of life were in the world outside. Well, the end of the year was coming soon and they'd be outside with these same men.

3

This change that gradually occurred in the most of our young seekers for truth is not to be explained by the simple fact that they were growing up. At least I don't think so. Nor by the old saying that familiarity breeds contempt. No, something else was happening. And in the meanwhile many of their fellows had fallen out of school. One by one they had left. And in some cases there had been accidents of piteous suicide. And it was not always for lack of money, or a sudden overpowering love affair or disappointment in a loyal promise or an early call of patriotism that caused so many of them to fall away. It was because of a vague and baffling discouragement which had begun to come over them, a chilling and invisible frost that blanched the tender greenery of their wishes and their dreams.

But we professors did all that we could to help them, did we not? We sympathized with them, talked to them, gave them quizzes written and oral, set them problems and projects in plenty to be solved, fed them with all the sterilized facts of a proved and scientific redemption. Semester after semester we taught them the tables, the graphs, and the symbolic configurations of time and space which proclaimed the universal law of cause and effect and the deterministic behavior of the universe and all that therein is. Did we not make them acquainted with the omnipotence of the fact, and the everlasting truth that is that fact—purged them with the calomel of many a knotty resultant and the bowel-erupting theorems of everlasting change? And yet even as we talked and labored with them so, some of them turned away their glances for a girl, or peered through the window at squirrels frisking on the ground, or listened to a gay uncaring fly buzzing by the window pane.

4

Indeed we did the best we could for them according to our lights and the precepts handed down forsooth from German scholarship, through the routine and ritual of facts, problems, and influences. But that was not enough. They wanted something besides facts and laws and the behavior of matter and things. They wanted something to believe in, something to move their souls, to help them keep their drive and increase it, something to lift their faith in themselves and the human race and a universal and benignant rightness which men call God. They wanted something that lived and moved and had its power beyond the reach of any analyses or compacted formulae. And we didn't give it to them. And life today is not the same rich invitation to them that it was when first they came into our care—

> With beaded bubbles winking at the brim
> And purple-stainèd mouth.

From what they tell me, from the letters I get, from the books and magazines I read, in last Sunday's *New York Times* even, too many of our young people are saying farewell to their professors in this time of leaf and fragrance, poorer than when they came. And poorer in the realest and most tragic way. Somebody, something, has hurt the wonder and the glory that once were theirs. Their enthusiasm has somehow been dimmed, their vision clouded. Doubts have sprung up in their mind. They are no longer so sure of their religion as once they were, or of the meaning of that widening stain upon the garment of the bruised and muted earth, or of their country, and perhaps least of all of themselves. This last is that which matters most.

5

So today up and down this land of ours—from California to Maine, from Puget Sound to Miami—thousands of them listen again to multitudinous graduation speakers of mellifluous or cacophonous words who try in the same old way and with the same old technique to pump them full of a fierce and fearful optimism. But they are tough nuts. They have been roiled and toiled and polished off by the educators and are hard to make an impression on. They know better. They have been to college. And besides, from all around them comes the clash of arms beating upon their ears. Something is violently wrong. And what they want as before is not advice and a discouraging list of facts, but a recharge of feeling and wild fresh impulse that once were theirs in the earlier fresher days— something to live for, something to fight for, something to die for. And these were what they'd come to us to find.

6

And why did they not find them? To call only a part of the blunt roll of reasons—we trained them in biology, that noble adventure of the free inquiring mind, known as the method and logic of vitality itself. But we set it forth as a problem whose secret was to be solved like a detective story and whose mystery lay in a minute gadget or thing hid in the dark. And so the coagulation of inclinations, the behavior of protoplasm under the microscope, was not enough.

And in that great superstition known as psychology, which for these many years has run rampant round the world, we hoped to give them help. We urged them there, we coaxed them there with all the devotion we could muster—covering the field from the prenatal mind, the libido, the ego, through insanity down to the id. And so they got to drinking a little before they'd come to class, or else sought comfort in the stray breathings of a poetic pessimism—

> Now and I muse for why and never find the reason,
> I pace the earth, and drink the air, and feel the sun.
> Be still, be still, my soul; it is but for a season:
> Let us endure an hour and see injustice done,

And in economics we gave them the concept of the monetary unit, the logic of goods and services, providing a policy of scrap iron to Japan on the one hand and a fund to China on the other to build air raid shelters from bombs made of this same scrap iron—to be obviously specific. For it was all part and parcel of the metaphysic of trade, we said. And morality and a pervading social responsibility, the joy even of human service, were none of its business or its part. So we taught them—to their present death in the jungles of the East. So through economics we showed them why most social maladjustments occur, how wars are fought for gain, heroes made, and ballads sung and written down. But that was not enough. We left out the ballad.

And in history and politics we taught them the rising and falling of nations and the chances therefor, but not the shameful and unethical reasons. And they wanted a clear compulsive apprehension of their own glorious democracy as a way of life. That we couldn't give them.

And in pedagogy, so often misnamed education, we provided them a complete case of terms—whether of medians and modes or quartile deviations—any and all and more like them to be used for living, or worse still to be visited on wayward-minded students whom they themselves might come to teach. And still the restlessness of their soul and the gloom of a too early winter night thickened above their head.

And in astronomy we gave them all that wealth and instruments could offer. And we hit them between the eyes with the findings of those instruments and calculations—that the universe is dying down. And if it is not dying down then it is according to other calculations swelling itself up like a great cosmic bladder to explode at some awful future date. In any case the outcome was to be disastrous for them, and there is no hope for ruined and pitiful man. But we did not teach them that the firmament sheweth the handiwork of God and that there is a benignity among the stars and a peace dropping therefrom like the gentle dew of evening. And how could we when the all-powerful and instrumented facts proved otherwise— namely, that they themselves were nothing but a speck of dust on a senseless wandering planet, a piece of dying protoplasm on the way out, and brief and powerless is their life? Over them, omnipotent matter holds her ceaseless sway, we recited from the authorities, and the slow doom of darkness and the certainty of the grave shall sweep them to death's oblivion. So thus we would take away their cowardice, their ignorance and fear, and as Bertrand Russell says, make them able to stand on their own feet self-reliant and affirmed for a triumphant stoic's life in the knowledge of the facts.

The list could be continued—even into the field of literature where we taught them more about sources, dates, categories of classification—than we did about the living art we studied. Yes, many an hour we spent showing them how Milton maybe used the wrong Latin ending in some of his poems—or the right one—and what historical and linguistic influences were at work upon him at that time, and rarely a word, never a gleam or fire-flash over his immortal poetry itself. And all the while they were starving for just that. Their eager minds were asking—but what have all these facts, these laws, these objective findings, got really to do with the great products of

man's poetic genius—except when so interpreted to keep
them from happening? Are any of the great works of
Dante, Michelangelo, Beethoven, Brahms, facts in such
a sense as this? These creations and others like them were
fired from the burning crucible of man's imagination,
and our purpose in studying them should be to receive
some of that fire and imagination into our own souls. This
they felt and knew. And the one way we had to keep that
from happening was to set them down in the valley of dry
bones gathering data and the facts.

7

These are the things and these are the ways most of us
college and university professors everywhere have taught
our young people—our citizens of a longed-for bright
tomorrow—the way we ourselves were taught in the pre-
ceding generation—filling their minds with generalities
and dead discouragement, miseducating them and making
them unfit to face the world they live in with any real
imagination, inspiration and hope. In that lovely old
ballad of the maid and the hawthorn tree the fable is to
the point—

> At last she askèd of the tree,
> How came this freshness unto thee
> And every branch so fair and clean?
> I marvel that you grow so green.
>
> The tree made answer by and by,
> I've cause to grow triumphantly,
> The sweetest dew that e'er was seen
> Doth fall on me to keep me green.

And this dewfall on the human spirit is the main and only matter, is it not?

It is a terrible confession to make, but I am sure that as our young students look back on their college career they will find that we professors have done a great deal—unwittingly we would say, but still we did it—to kill whatever enthusiasm, whatever delight, whatever of beauty they used to see in the world. Thank God there are exceptions. I had one of them for a teacher. And when I remember the courses I took with him twenty-one years ago, I don't recall the facts he taught me about Wordsworth for instance. What I do remember and still feel across this expanse of years is the emotion, the infectious spirit of his teaching. He experienced Wordsworth, lived in him as he taught him, and I shared in that experience— vital, warm, and illuminating. I can still see him as he looked out over his class, his eyes full of vigor and joy, his voice vibrant and touched with passion and the feeling of that which we read—

> It is a beauteous evening calm and free,
> The holy time is quiet as a nun
> Breathless with adoration; ...
> Listen! The mighty Being is awake,
> And doth with his eternal motion make
> A sound like thunder—everlastingly.

And a thrill would run through me, it still does. Or again—

> There was a time when meadow, grove and stream,
> The earth and every common sight
> To me did seem
> Apparelled in celestial light,
> The glory and the freshness of a dream.

And I live again that rich eternal hour, know again that my redeemer liveth still, beyond the reach of time or clutch of tool, or blood and war, and formulated circumstances.

8

But this failure has not been our fault entirely, we would plead. For so we were done to by others who preceded us. Have we not all been misled by the fair schematism of science which for so long has seemed to offer the provable way to salvation? This kind of frustration has happened before. The scholasticism of the middle ages once held Europe and all culture in its grip. But there also too many clamorous hearts kept crying out against an empty wordage of sacred authority and diluted intuition, and finally beauty, enthusiasm, and the Renaissance arrived again. Then the revulsion completed itself. And from Copernicus, Galileo, Newton, Bacon, Darwin, and Edison down the pendulum has swung the other way. And now it is near the point where it ought to stop—to use a clockmaker's figure. Can we professors help it stop? For the world has begun to realize that science offers no substitute for a full way of life—of religion and of beauty. China has known this for thousands of years, though it invented gunpowder. The truth, the beauty which all men crave, including professors, and lacking which they die in blindness, is not to be found hidden behind an onion peel of fact or any experimental test. It is identical with being a man, and men everywhere instinctively know this is true just as they did in younger days. Every seer, every poet, every lover, even those men who glimpsed the future destiny of this country a hundred and seventy-five years ago—some of them—have spoken it forth in living words. To paraphrase the great Italian philosopher Benedetto Croce—

What we seek and enjoy in life, what makes our hearts leap up and ravishes our admiration is the joy, the movement, the passion, the fire, the feeling of the living soul. These alone give us the supreme criterion for distinguishing the true from the false; inspiration from failure; lack from fulfillment.

In short and simple terms—we professors, we keepers of wisdom, following the pragmatic bent of the times, not guiding it as we are sworn to do—have lost our religion, our inspiration for living, and with us lies the responsibility most for what our young people are and may be. If this is true, and I believe it is, then are we not responsible also for much of the present tragedy in the world itself?

For this latter crime cannot be charged upon the helpless animals, or the flowers, the stones, rivers, the trees and hills, can it? No. Nature continues its everlasting miracle of birth, fruitage, and yielding to change without responsibility there. Only men themselves have brought this woe and suffering upon themselves. And why? Because of the thoughts that worked within them to frustration. And who were the shapers of these thoughts? Who taught them, who controlled them in the most poetic and formative period of their development in the days gone by? We their teachers did.

And now that the world lies enveloped in the sinner's bed of pain which we helped prepare, there is much contrite talk about the new day of convalescence and the sweet morn of healing to be. And that such a time should come few of us will argue. The summons to reform grows more demanding. Will we as teachers participate in that new day and bring to bear upon it something of stimulating drive and direction, or will we repeat our failure as before? Now for the first time in the three hundred and fifty years of our American history the cultural and spiritual leadership of the world is in our care. This added opportunity and privilege have come to us. Art, literature, music, drama, true science, philosophy, and all the noblest creations of man's genius are dislodged and beaten almost beyond surviving there in Europe and Asia—where once was built their dwelling place, their haven and their home.

Then it is up to us to provide them a new home, a fane for their worship, a sheltering cathedral over them. Ours is now the chance to cherish them, refurnish them and renew them, add our bit to their development and growth and so endow them with greater richness and wonder for those who shall come after us. This too is a sacred trust we have to hold. Can we then as called defenders of a wider realm than any sea or slant of land pledge ourselves to a new devotion in the cause we claim to serve and the faith we should profess? Will we as individuals in the all-embracing democracy of the spirit accept the teacher's responsibility in this the higher program of victory? As the artist must paint and shape more and better now than ever before for the time allowed him, the composer sound more perfectly the music in his heart, the poet seek more zealously for the heat and flame of his inspiration, the statesman for the social truth which is the human truth, so should the teacher strive with all honesty and imagination to make manifest in living eager hearts the whole of these. For these are the inner springs of man's promise and his

fulfillment. These are what give color, energy, and abiding value to the earth. Save them and the new day of justice, peace, and brotherhood for which our young men
die will likely save itself. Lose them and barbarity comes
again.

Will we do this? Will we measure up to this challenge
that stands squarely before us? Or will we continue our
dry and spiritless purveying of empty authority, of dull
and unsublimated fact, in the ruined and barren stalls of
life? Have we the reserve of character in all humility to
confess our failure heretofore, the potential courage and
vision to regenerate ourselves as men for the new need and
the new generation, and rise up and give ourselves with
fervor and whole heart to the cause of a deeper faith—of
truth and beauty and wisdom of the human soul? If we
cannot, if we will not, then it were better that our calling
be abolished and every Ph. D. of us set to cleaning the
guns, or hauling trash, or dozing in the sun out of life and
harm's way.

For in sweeping affirmation, it ought to be a glorious
thing to be born into this world. And it is, no matter what
the man-made conditions of that world may be at any
given time, or what we tell of it in our uncouth and aca-
demic vocabularies. For here is the habitation and the
home of enthusiasm and joy if we but witness it—of the
ever shining goal ahead, of wonder and the dream. In our
youth we feel it true, every instinct of our beating hearts
declares it. And the passing days with all their learning
and their lore should confirm and not deny it. And, to repeat, if these techniques and methodologies of the
teachers, their *sine qua* questionings and dark divinings,
their conflicting creeds and instrumental findings add but

to confusion and despair among men, then something is badly wrong with both the teacher and his teaching.

What will we do about these things? What new curriculum will we offer for an ancient and eternal need?

The Artist's Challenge

1

THE ETERNAL IDEAL OF THE BEAUTIFUL HAS CEASE-lessly haunted the human race, and man through the ages has sought to fashion his life in terms of that ideal. But betrayed by his own appetites, weakened and confused by false doctrines and nightmares of dread, and hindered and handicapped by many an evil chance and accident of fortune and war, he has too often failed in this seeking and too rarely succeeded. But still his effort to build an ever more noble life goes on, and will go on until the scientific universe has swallowed him and his dream to nothingness or until he has won something of the final and ultimate victory. The eventuality of the former is the business of omnipotent and necessitous nature, but the possibility of the latter is all his concern and his alone. In this his destiny as a man is fixed, and to yield up the struggle like a clod or complacent animal is to invite the death from which there is no resurrection.

17

By the very nature of his being man is a living soul and not an animal. The first act of thinking is to declare it. And as a living soul, a spirit, he is a creator, a maker, an artist. His life itself is an effort in creation. From his birth to his death he shapes fair forms where there were none. He makes his songs even in tongueless silence, and builds his shining structures among the wayward sticks and stones— even from these sticks and stones. He begets life in the midst of death, and as a prophet sings of hope among the omens of doom. So does he forever try to find and fashion forth that ideal of perfection which haunts him from the cradle to the grave. So does he endlessly create new products of that ideal, being himself a new creation beyond all accounting for out of time and space, and in his intent like the Power itself that first created him. And he carries in his heart the divine imperative of the Maker's will from whence he came. This is once more his glory and vindication for being born, this the rich rewarding for the enthralling burden of his days.

And down the stretchy path of history behind him, he has left the tokens and witnesses of this fact. Many a temple, tomb, shrine, book, picture, song, statue, bridge, road, or invention he has reared in proud and ecstatic affirmation of the findings on his noble quest. And here and there, however far apart they be, have been ages, periods of time when the inspiration of the ideal has seized upon and fired him not separate and alone but in whole communities and groups of men alike. And the single prophetic voice, the single pair of valiant hands have been joined by other voices and other pairs of hands and a mighty concerted effort of creation set to work. Then it was those cultures and bodies of corporate beauty were

erected which still remain to us living and real and un-
corrupted by corroding time. Through them the past was
made manifest in meaning and the future had its hope. In
any roll call today they still declare their truth.

2

The Chaldean seers, brooding on the wide, inscrutable
sky, found in the mystic signs and configurations written
in the stars a message of care and purpose for the human
race. And in their books of stone they put their readings
down, and for generations men were gladdened and en-
couraged on their way because of them. The Egyptian
builders with their pyramids and ponderous temples
glimpsed the eternality of life that lives through and beyond death, and they avowed their buoyant hope even in
the grave, even in the tokens of the scented cerement, the
mummy, and the bull. And the sages and poets of China,
out of darkness, flood, and hunger, envisioned the kingdom celestial and radiant on high and man's citizenship
in that kingdom. The Brahmin gazed upon the everlasting
blindness and emptiness of space and found not death
there but a principle of fertility and beneficence to man.
And he sang it forth in his divine books for us to draw
comfort from—the Vedas and Upanishads.
The Persians, too, witnessed the weary round of the
setting sun and the falling night and discovered not frustration and hopelessness in that iteration but the logic of
man's soul ever renewing itself in light unquenchable, a
mystery to be celebrated and adored. The Buddhists in
their ceaseless search through the tangle of sin and pain
arrived at the eight-fold way and the soul's peace in wor-

shipful contemplation along that way. The Jewish wanderer through long wilderness trials and sufferings finally found his abiding place in Canaan Land, and in thanksgiving and praise avowed his Lord of Hosts above, who reigned in majesty and glory and whose beauty was like the eyelids of the morning. And the piteous Jesus and His disciples, treading the sharp shards of Golgotha, sang above their bleeding feet of the gift of love and humility of men. The Greek in his rocky and arid hills created the fable of the dawn-beautiful world of grace and symmetry, of measure and balance, where luminous men and women, gods and goddesses, walked in his own ideal of the beautiful, the noble, and the true. The knight of the middle ages, burning with the vision of the shining grail, rode to face death and all unimaginable terrors in demon-infested forests, ogre-haunted caverns and mountains, as he strove to find the emblem of his yearning and bring it home.

And in Elizabethan England Shakespeare and his fellows sang in lyric poems and plays of the wonder of a new-awakened age, the glory of far empires and adventures of strong imaginative men ruling and exploring the earth and marking out its boundaries, and the sublimity of the moral order over them. The poet-scientists then in this same England found the law which asserted that the smallest and dullest fragment of matter, the ultimate point of space, and the last instant of time are not soulless and inchoate things but are permeated by the universal relationship and meaning of the whole. Nothing is excepted whether of matter, space, or time, they said, and all that exists is beholden to this power, is haunted by the ideal of harmony and beauty.

And in that rich musical century in Germany, the creative spirit of man working in Bach, Mozart, and Beethoven sang forth as never before or since its hymns and dithyrambs, its melody and harmony, telling of the hopes and dreams of the human race and the ideal of beauty and the perfect order. And even in the natural world of physical vitality itself Darwin, Wallace, Huxley, and Spencer broke the riddle open and found again this same ideal of perfection and upward climb at work, a self-improvement moving towards the ever-beckoning goal. So the story has gone.

3

These have been some of the great ages, the mountain peaks of man's experience and his effort. And though many a wide valley of desolation and dry bones may lie between, it is only the mountain peaks that mark for us the geography of that wide discovered land, it is only they our imagination feeds upon, and they alone as it were which have tongues to speak to us of inspiration and the dream. The rest is silence and forgetfulness. And on these mountain tops the beacon fires lighted long ago by vanished hands still burn for us. And as they illumine the darkness of the past so do they cast their gleam a little way along the path we have to go and where we too shall build our mountain peaks and light our fires as witnesses to the creative spirit for those that shall come after us— where we shall build them if we will.

In each of these times and deeds of accomplishments the adjurement and the theme have always been the same —man in search of his ideal. The inner voice speaks it clear for all to hear, echoes the truth that lives in all men's souls—saying: "In the beginning was the Word, and the Word was with God, and the Word was God. The same was in the beginning with God. . . . And the Word was made flesh, and dwelt among us, and we beheld his glory, the glory as of the only begotten of the Father, full of grace and truth." And when an age, an individual have ceased to listen to this voice, have weakened in the search, given over the divine prerogative and yielded to sloth and fatness of days, to despair or denial, they have perished without exception and with no memorial of meaning to tell that they had been.

The poets and the prophets, the singers, the rightful builders and the priests have repeated this theme from generation to generation. For there is no other real theme to repeat and should be none. With Plato they have said: "Man must learn to use the beauties of earth as steps along which he mounts upward, going from fair forms to fair practices, and from fair practices to fair notions, until from fair notions he arrives at the notion of absolute beauty, and at last knows what the essence of beauty is. . . . If man has eyes to see the true beauty, he becomes the friend of God and immortal." With Hegel they reiterate that "Art and the creation of art, being works which originate in and are begotten of the spirit, are themselves stamped with the hallmark of spirit."

And with Nietzsche they assert: "Art is essentially affirmation, benediction, deification of existence. The artist's function is the invention and arrangement of a world in which we affirm ourselves in our inmost needs. The artist makes artists of all who can appreciate his mes-

sage. Works of art arouse the condition which creates art."
And with Eugene Veron they declare: "Art, from being
the blossom and fruit of civilization, is rather its germ. . . .
Art is the direct and spontaneous manifestation of human
personality."

4

Such is the doctrine of man the idealist, of man the
artist and creator. And even in this present hour when
the followers of brutal might and the iron fist are abroad
in the world declaring otherwise, we are the more certain
of its truth. For it is a proof of the blindness and degradation of these men, whatever their nationality, that they
offer force instead of love, the fist instead of the friendly
enclosing hand. From the valley of their confusion and
despair the dictators, their converts and imitators proclaim that "Ideas such as democracy, conscience of the
world, internationality of art breed cowardice." From
their puppet podiums they shout that by strength of national arms "blood and race will once more become the
source of artistic intuition" and a new world will be built
by these fresh Aryan hands. In their folly they denounce
as weaknesses the virtues that normal healthy-minded
men instinctively crave everywhere—kindliness, brotherhood, love for one another, mutual kinship as aspiring
beings seeking for the same perfection and traveling
down the same long way together, irrespective of race
or creed.

For the dictators and their diseased followers such
principles as these are but sickly phantasms of a supersti-
tious and outmoded time, and are to be destroyed, will be

destroyed whenever and wherever they meet the triumphant march of the sons of force. So they say and continue
to say even as their undoing draws quickly on, even as the
grotesque impedance they would seek to lay across the
path of progress is being shouldered away.

This is the old story of man's frailty and his failure.
There have been other dictators and other hordes of heavy-
footed men in other ages who have tried to flaunt the everlasting truth by which humanity lives and has its being.
They have often for a while succeeded in disrupting the
fated flow and will of things, but not for long. And as they
substitute the sword and the rifle for the bible and the
song, just so in the end do these same instruments render
a mocking requiem over them. And the only light to shine
above their wordless grave today is shed from those same
beacon fires they in their madness so futilely tried to
quench.

For it is an obvious thing that power and force, armies
raised and battles fought, speeches declaimed and practices indulged in are useless and empty of meaning if they
stand as enemies over against the eternal ideal. They never
succeed in their final intent and never can. The moral
nature of man in the large always rebels against them,
always casts them out and reapplies itself after each inter-
ruption to the one and only task. And that task is not the
avaunting of one individual or one group of men or nation
in power over another, but the lifting up of all men together. Or as the creative spirit puts it—the fashioning of
an ever more perfect world in which all men should share.
We know this instinctively as joyful and true, and the
unforgivable evil, the unpardonable sin against this privi-

lege and principle is to cease to remember it, is to cease
to struggle for it.

Such is the demand of a real democracy.

5

And so the message has run through the ages like a
musical theme in the symphony of life, or like a beacon
flashed from mountain top to succeeding mountain top.
And always the voice of the poet, the artist, the creator has
spoken the summons clearest, has held the torch farthest
aloft. Now in our own land our poets and singers, following Whitman, here and there have caught the song, have
seen the gleam, and are adding their word to the universal
proclamation, their spark of fire to the eternal flame. And
what we need now is more poets, more than ever before—
more singers, more laborers in the vineyard of this our
one true Lord. And only when we've got them can we hope
to swell the scattered jubilate, the individual *te deum* into
an inspiring chorus sounding again the everlasting refrain
of man's divine search for his haven and his home. Only
thus can we create here in these United States another of
the mountain peak times with their quenchless flame
which it is our duty to create.

A hundred and seventy-five years ago our forefathers
laid the foundation and the hope for such an age in their
basic principles of the free and democratic man. With that
as a beginning we should erect here one of the inspiring
epochs of history. That is our challenge and the one challenge we must not fail to meet. And all of us as workers,
however humble—whether poets, singers, builders, paint-
ers, philosophers, dramatists, producers of plays, or sol-

diers—carry the answer in ourselves. For all of us without exception are haunted by the eternal ideal of the beautiful. In that, all of us are artists, creators. Then let us declare it true and create.

We will. We have already started.

Drama And The Weather

IF YOU'VE EVER BEEN DOWN IN THE COUNTRY DURING
a severe summer drought, you have noticed how the crops
stood lifeless and how the leaves and limbs of the trees
sagged under the wilting heat, and how the chickens in the
barnyard sat slothfully on the ground, and the cattle in
the shadow of the buildings looked out at the world with
dull and inert eyes. The farmers themselves seemed testy
and irritable about the house, and with reason, for day
after day the sun has risen like a ball of fire, swum across
the brazen empty sky and gone down beyond the rim of
brown hills—a fiery curse to animal, earth, and man. The
world itself is perishing for rain, but there is no rain.

Then one morning a different feeling is in the air. After
breakfast you walk in the lane, and a change is over everything. The flowers and the trees have perked up their heads,
the chickens step about lively, and the pigeons no longer
quarrel under the eaves. Down in the pasture the cattle

27

move brisky around biting off green willow tips, and the farmer and his sons are long ago abroad looking to their dikes and ditches. You go down to the village for the mail. More than once you hear a store loafer say, "The air feels like rain." Being a summer boarder, you read the morning papers, then an article or two in a magazine about trouble in Europe, and after lunch sit on the front porch and take a rest.

Looking off across the burning fields about two o'clock, you see low on the horizon edge a faint little wad of cloud, no larger than the cloud Elijah or Polonius saw. And as you sit there watching, another little cloud appears swimming up the sky, to be followed by another and then another. Soon the whole southwestern horizon is marked by these little upboiling racks. And in less time than it takes to tell, a low dark swollen band begins shoving itself up behind them and above the line of sycamore trees along the river. Presently there is a roll of low ominous thunder below the earth, and the windows rattle in their sockets.

The moments pass, the dark wide stretching cloud now reaches from north to south and pushes up until it touches the edge of the burning sun. Then it obscures the sun. A flash of lightning marks a sudden fiery crack from sky to earth. The elm trees around the house shiver with a strange delight. The chickens start going into the henhouse and the doves fly into their cote. And then up from the meadow the old bell-cow comes leading the other cattle, her head high, her tail arched merrily.

Another roll of thunder sounds, a gust of dust cuts a little jigging whirlwind swift down the lane, trying to keep up with the edge of the cloud which now has raced across

the sky and passed over the house. The wind blows more
strongly, and somewhere a door slams. You continue to
sit, waiting for the rain to fall. The wind dies out, the
thunder is no longer heard, nor is there any lightning.
Everything is breathless, expectant, still.

Now with a sudden clatter like stones on the roof or
gravel thrown, the rain begins. A fine mist of dust is beat
up in the yard, and in the lane and out across the fields.
Like a morning ground-fog it is. And then it too is wetted
down to earth as the rain settles into a steady pour. A
sheet of wetness begins to blow in on you, and the air is
full of a rich sodden, loamy smell. You pick up your
chair, lean it against the wall, and enter the house. There
you stand by the window looking out where a world is
being refreshed and where a snake of yellow water has
started wriggling down the dry road ditch. The drought
is over. In a few days everything will be green again.

There was once an old question as to who could chart the
winds and the nature thereof and who could foretell the
weather and its whims. The question still stands today un-
answered as it did in Job's time. No doubt there are laws
governing all such phenomena, and maybe someday these
laws will be understood—laws that have no irrational
phantom dancing within them. But even so those who
understand will have no power to bring either drought or
rain, for the wind will still blow where it listeth and it will
rain when it will rain.

And as with the weather, so with writing a play—so
with any work of art. It comes pretty much when it will
come, is absent when it will be absent, and no man can
provide its presence at his will. So if I may be personal in
replying to your question, "Why do you write plays," I

can on first consideration easily say, "I don't know." It is much like the weather to me—the what and why, the wherefore and results. About the only answer I would venture is that I seem to need to. If I were certain that the drama were the one means of gaining honor or wealth or mental stability there would be some obvious sense in spending one's life trying to set down lines for people to speak on a stage. I believe I should want to write plays, though, if little or nothing came of them, but naturally I want a lot to come of them.

Of course your question goes further than any easy answer or any meteorological metaphor. It raises the whole problem of aptitude and calling. I think all people are by nature artists, that is, more or less so. The usual European designation of the American builder and business man as a money hog, for instance—a creature who takes pleasure only in dollar profit and pain only in dollar loss—seems to me obviously false. There is more to it than that—always more. Sinclair Lewis in one of his novels, *Work of Art*, tries his hand at showing that one Myron Weagle with his dream of a perfect hotel might be considered essentially an artist. There is a lot of human truth in his contention.

Now if all of us have this so-called artistic urge, then why do some of us become hotel keepers and others banjopickers or playwrights? That is the next question. The answer is perhaps that circumstances always play their part. One child happens to have access, say, to a piano near at hand but finds his fingers too stiff or too short ever to allow of his becoming a performer. Perhaps he turns to composing, or bricklaying. And so it goes. Each of us could make some sort of statement as to his proper calling.

Take your own case—you run a drama magazine. All sorts of odds and ends of circumstances and people went into your choice of that career.

Two incidents happened to me years ago, I remember, which turned me to writing plays. Norman Foerster, who was one of the finest English teachers ever to appear at the University of North Carolina, announced in class one day that the seniors had decided to do a play at Commencement and were holding a contest for original scripts. He advised me to try my hand. I took a chance at the thing and happened to win out. The play was produced in the forest theatre and I was thrilled to death. After that though I didn't set my heart on playwriting, for I had always been more interested in poetry and short stories than anything else. Then in 1919 "Proff" Koch came riding in from the Dakota prairies, his arms full of plays and his head full of dreams. In no time a stage was up, and everybody near and far, little and big, black and white realized for the first time that he, said body, was an artist of some sort —mainly a dramatic artist. Some went in for designing, some for acting, some for writing. I chose the last. And after a few productions, I was caught fast in my choice and had struck acquaintance with all the bat-like terrors that inhabit the shadows of the stage.

Your next question is easier to answer. "Why do you write the plays you do?" The answer is—that's the only kind I know how to write. Most of the plays I have written can be designated as folk plays, and I know this seems a narrow boundary. Perhaps it is, but since the "folk" are the people who seem to matter most to me, I have little interest in trying to deal with others who are more foreign and therefore less real to me. Not for a moment do I claim to have done justice to an inspiring subject matter, but the challenge is there, clearer, sharper, and more compelling every day. For there is something in the life of "the people" which seems of deeper significance so far as the nature of the universe goes than the characters who might be termed sophisticated. To examine the matter a little further, it seems to me that the folk are those living closer to a terrible and all-wise nature than their brethren of the sidewalks and opera house, and if I were seeking a philosophical statement for the matter it would be somewhat as follows:

The folk are the people whose manners, ethics, religious and philosophical ideals are more nearly derived from and controlled by the ways of the outside physical world (Cf. Synge's *Riders to the Sea*) than by the ways and institutions of men in a specialized society (Cf. Schnitzler's *Anatol* cycle). And the outside natural world is the fountain of wisdom, the home of the fruitful all-mother, the omnipotent God. The line of demarcation between the folk and sophisticated drama is not always easily contrasted; to instance once more, Ferenc Molnar's *The Guardsman* and S. Ansky's *The Dybbuk*. And between the last two I'd always choose *The Dybbuk*—even though technique should shift for itself.

I don't claim that sophisticated drama may not be great in its own right, but somehow I never thrill to it as I do to what I like to term the folk drama the Greeks wrote, the kind Shakespeare and Tolstoi and Hauptmann wrote; the kind Alexis Granowsky used to produce in Russia with its lovely burden of folk imagery, music and song. In reading *Lear*, for example, I always feel a sudden lift when we come to the heath scene. There is something grand and universal in the naked relationship of the old king to the powers of nature around him.

And as characters available to art purposes, to repeat, those who live as it were with their feet in the earth and their heads bare to the storms, the lightning and the gale— those who labor with their hands wresting from cryptic nature her goods and stores of sustenance—these develop a wisdom of living which seems to me more real and beautiful than those who develop their values and ambitions from rubbing shoulders in a crowded city.

And that wisdom it is which seems important—a wisdom which is a consciousness of the great eternal Presence by which men live and move and have their being and without which they die. And if the playwrights who tell of captains and lords, kings and queens, dolls and manikins, can open up the doors of crowded buildings, cut through the filmy arras that conceals our human instincts and hopes and fears and go to the first principles of human identity—then they raise the hair on our heads too with their voice from the sacred grove of Colonus. And no longer do we think of man as sophisticated or folk, but man—man alone with his God and his destiny. And when this happens—and rare is Shakespeare, rarer than the Phoenix—then the matter is all one and listeners are all one.

But the present clang and confusion of wheel on iron, yelling and clamor of tickers and tellers, the secrecy of vaults and locks and braggarty monoliths of incorruptible concrete and steel—these all make it harder for us to see and hear the God who is the principle of our lives. Maybe I'm crazy on the idea of God, but then aren't we all? I refer to the wild pell mell rush every evening out of the city to the country—to the country where the birds are, where the grass is and where there is peace or should be.

Now you catch me almost carrying on into a scheme of social philosophy. And if I wanted to apply this half-surmised esthetic theory to the control and arrangement of peoples I should say there ought to be plenty of trees and land and outdoors for every man. For only in the outdoors can we associate with power and mystery in their most sublime manifestation. And heaven knows we ought to sense in any way we can whatever touch of sublimity there may be vouchsafed unto us in this darkness.

Now it seems that after all I'm saying for myself that folk-drama as such is or can be more significant than sophisticated drama. Not at all. I mean to repeat that in the last analysis it is a question of neither folk nor sophisticate—but of man, man in his environment, and it is in the main a matter for the poet, the creator, the seer. And I would say that indoors sooner or later man must perish and outdoors there is more of a chance for him.

To make another dogmatic statement, I would say that cruelty, scorn, and evils of all sorts are more native to the great cities than not, and therefore we should be better off without any great cities—I mean close, skyscraper, bedlam cities. (There's something other than politics behind Russia's efforts to create the ideal commune). And all the little towns that get too large for their britches and so full of metropolital urges and apings that they cut down all the trees on their main streets and cover the grass and ground with concrete will be better off when they tear up the concrete, reset the trees, and grow grass again. And maybe now that we have evolved wheels and telephones and radios and machinery of long-distance coöperation of all sorts we can all begin to live more among flowers and trees again and yet keep in touch with each other enough for our sophisticated needs. Then haply now and again we may also have a word with the Great Presence where He walks by the river bank at evening.

As to your next question of "What happens when you turn your play over to the director, designer, actor, and see them add their form to yours?"—it is more than easy to say that sometimes you are pleased with what they do and sometimes disappointed. It is never possible for the image-picture of your characters to be entirely duplicated on the stage. Their habits, their actions and appearance are always different and necessarily so. But I think the production as often improves the play over the author's mind as it is likely to hurt it—that is, a good production.

Your last question as to what the playwright should be to the theatre and to the world he lives in opens up a huge wheel-full of diverging thoughts. Briefly though, he should be, don't you think, the same to the theatre as the gardener to his garden, or the blacksmith to his smithy, and the carpenter to his house? And as for the world he lives in— his business is simply to express in dramatic form the human struggles, both evil and good, that exist in that world. In Aristotelian phrase, he is a maker, and his business is to fashion or make his material fit the imaginative demands of his craft. But how wonderfully difficult it is and how joyful! How like the weather, like the rain!

And in these two words of material and craft all the trouble lies, of course. But the trouble is not final, however mysterious and difficult the matter is—do you think so? For in the great outside universe around us nature is always solving these dualistic antagonisms, whether it be raining or whether it be dry, and from her we may no doubt derive both the axiom and the dream.

It occurs to me that I make no place for comedy (which includes melodrama and farce). Well, it apparently belongs to another point of view, just as the grotesque requires still a third kind of judgment. Comedy seeks to belong entirely to man's world and to have no place in nature's world. In fact one might say that it arises from man's delight in prankishness with himself and fellow-man in so far as he forgets that he is a part of an all-powerful and demanding universe. Its basic pattern is a non-harmful incongruity which man himself provides, and that would seem to justify the definition. For nature is never funny nor playful, not even when she smiles, is she?

As for the grotesque (the hysterical), it disappears before definition and stands representative of nothing more than the frightful effort to combine the comic and the sublime (or the finite funny with the infinite serious) into the body of one piece.

You see, your letter has stirred up a whole hornet's nest of trouble for me. And now that I've had to take refuge in the quagmire of metaphysics, I'd better stop. So I'll conclude by—yes, I'll say it—the play's the thing after all, whether it's indoors or outdoors—but like the weather it is most outdoors.

The Theatre And The Screen

1

Y EARS AGO I STOOD WITH MY FATHER IN A SIDE SHOW and saw a miracle happen on a screen. A little man in a top hat was shown diving from a high platform into a swimming pool and then springing backwards out of the water and up onto his perch again. The tent that day was crowded with farmers and their wives and children who had come to see the sword swallower and the wild man from Borneo. But when for the last act this jerky little figure came walking along the side of the tent as it were, made his manikin bow to us the audience and then went twirling down from his high perch into the water, and zoop! back again the way he'd come, we thought no more of smoking knives or bloody meat that day. Later at night the farmers, their wives and children, all on the roads that led home like lengthening spokes from the bright city to the rim of darkness were talking of this wonder.

"But the thing moved like a real man, Mommee."

"So it did move. It was a man."

"How did they make it move like that?"

"You tell him, George."

"How did they, Poppee?"

"Edison and such fellows can do anything these days."

"But he dived somersaults backwards and up in the air, I bet twenty feet."

"Them fellows are smart, I tell you."

"But Poppee—A man can't really do that, can he, Poppee?"

"Go to sleep, son, I tell you."

2

In 1915 *The Birth of a Nation* came to our capital city. The newspapers and wayside signs worked up a lot of interest in our section, and I rode off to see it. After a trip of several hours over thirty-five miles of miry road, I arrived at the crowded theatre door and finally made my way inside and up into the balcony. Now every seat in the house was taken. The lights went down, the orchestra began to play, and things started to happen. It would be hard to describe the effect of the picture on that audience. There on the screen in front of our eyes not more than twenty yards away we saw brave armies fighting as only brave ones can. We heard the roar of cannon, the neighing of horses, saw the bleeding and the dying, the fluttering flags and banners. And all the while the thunder and beat of the orchestra whipped our souls along in the story. Now like a breath the tumult is gone, the rumble and cannonading die out and a beautiful woodland vision entrances us. There stands the handsome Little Colonel and his exquisite

Southern sweetheart, dove in hand and all, saying a fond farewell, and the music of the violin proclaims the piteousness of their love. Then with a flick the scene has changed again, and we see the dark and sliding figure of the villain prowling around a vine-clad cottage, and the evil of his nature is intensified for us in the croompy notes of the bassoons.

So the story went on unfolding, in dumb show and musical sound, the hopes, the loves, and the dangers that beset these our heroic characters. The audience sat one moment in breathless anxiety, another moment they were applauding the short triumph of virtue and honor. And when at last the robed and wind-blown figure of the Klansman on his horse stood in a medium close-up on a hill, and the bugle in the orchestra announced with its high note that a stern and powerful force of righteousness was risen to defend the innocent ones from all villains of whatsoever creed or color, a frenzy ran among the spectators like fire among broomstraw. There were yells and shouts, clenching of fists, and loud unashamed oaths. One woman directly in front of me sprang up as in a religious hysteria and screamed, "Kill 'em, Kill 'em!" and then like a lady in a play or protracted meeting fell with a fainting thud to the floor. One of the ushers hurried up and carried her out, but even as he went he kept looking back towards the screen. (Not until years later did I realize that without the bugle note the lady would not have fainted. It was then I got my theory of music in the theatre, of symphonic drama.)

I saw *The Birth of a Nation* many times, and its effect on the audience was always much the same. True, these audiences were Southern, and this would account for some

of the emotional outbursts on racial matters, but from
general reports this film was a great success in all parts of
the world. (I should like to mention here that of all the
modern stage plays I have witnessed or heard about none
of them seem to have affected the audience to the degree
that this melodramatic and romantic story did.)

The next event in the movies for me was Charlie
Chaplin. One day in 191. his *Shoulder Arms* was shown in
a French cantonment for us American soldiers. Here again
the audience was moved to vent its loud appreciation.
Chuckles and gales of laughter swept through the hall at
the antics of the little man, and for a while the memory of
air raids, whining 75's, snipers, stink and filth was forgotten. He was the divine magician playing with the
bauble of our souls for an hour. And some weeks later,
when I saw the likeness of Charlot hauled through the
streets of Paris and followed by a great crowd of hurrah-
ing boys and girls, I joined in the procession which led
to a moving-picture entrance. And from that day to this I
have followed wherever he leads. A few years ago I sat
with a friend who, like me, was seeing "The Gold Rush"
for the tenth time. After the show we spoke in guilty
defense of Shakespeare and the drama and felt sad that
neither of us would wish to see one of those plays ten
times. But the afterthought that we had read most of
Shakespeare's plays more than ten times and would continue to read them comforted us where thoughts of the
stage could not.

Who would try to explain Chaplin's great appeal to the
world—an appeal that would doubtless be lost in a medium other than the movies? And, so far as I know, no actor
in the theatre has ever been so generally effigied, honored,

and adored. Even his shoes and cane and every bit of costume are destined to some sort of immortality somehow and somewhere—or should be. He is the first great genius of the film. His creations as actor, scenarist, and director outweigh all that has been done either by the beauties and bores of Hollywood or by Griffith, Eisenstein, Pabst, Pudovkin, or Clair. And when this is said, the inspired work of the great German actor, Emil Jannings, and our own Walt Disney is not forgot. Chaplin is the pioneer pointing the way, and he has already provided us with the technique for future progress. Disney follows him.

3

Some time ago I had the chance to do some movie writing in Hollywood. With all the glaring evidence of cheap pictures that fill the world before me, and with plenty of warnings against Babylon and all its waste and iniquities, I landed at one of the major studios. This at last was the glittering world of Pirandellian make-believe, where everything seems what it is not and yet is what it seems. Here were hundreds of acres of buildings where dreams were manufactured, where thousands of people went in and out early and late creating millions of feet of film on which were imprinted little shadows which, placed against a steady light, acted, talked, and danced and spun their thousand-and-one tales of ambition, love, hope, or despair.

The first thing to do was to see inside and get acquainted with the goings-on. And so I did, and tried to understand what I saw. I read all the books on the movies I could get— both European and American. I poked about in the cutting rooms, the wardrobes, the projection rooms and construction departments. I read the engineers' handbooks on light and sound devices. I made myself familiar with all the camera terms from "angle-shot" to "wipe-off." And the more I learned the more enthusiastic I became. Here indeed was the creation of the machine age which was the equal of the Word as spoken by men of old. Here was a medium infinite and universal in its power, able to depict anything—whether in heaven, or earth, or in hell; whether of man's relation to man or man's deepest submerged self. For the first time in history a completely democratic art form was available, capable of answering any vital demand made upon it by the imagination of any human being. For the first time in the history of the world we had a dramatic medium in the movies which could be understood by black and white, yellow or red, the only requirement being that the audience must be able to see or hear— better if it could do both. For pantomime is and can be understood by all men of whatever race, creed, or calling, and music likewise. A Japanese will laugh at Charlie Chaplin even as a New Yorker will.

For several weeks I labored on a script, trying to measure up in some degree to the camera which was to express the story I had to tell. No one hurried me, nobody said do this or that. Apparently I was left free to do as I chose. What was this nonsense I had heard about the cramping power of Hollywood and its slave-driving methods with writers? I began to doubt tales of woe which brethren of my kind had been wont to tell. At last my script was in some sort of final shape, and conferences with producer, director, leading actor, and men of the technical staff began. The scenario was read, discussed, and tentatively accepted. I was pleased to find that the boss men said only a little revision was needed here and there and the thing would be ready for shooting. The revisions suggested seemed sensible enough, and I gladly tried to make them. So the script was finally delivered into the producer's hands, and I began another job while it was being shot. Now and then, I would hear a report from the lot that "everything was going fine," and I was beginning to feel some pride in the fact that this picture was to be a little better maybe than the general Hollywood product. A few times I went on the set and watched the making and came away with nothing but admiration for the studio and its employees. How hard and seriously everybody seemed to be working—from early morning till late at night they labored. And as time went on I learned that, contrary to general report, hard work was the rule in Hollywood. Nervous breakdowns there are not all liquor and libidos.

When the picture was finally completed, I went down town to see it. It turned out to be a straightforward, level, and unimpressive thing. Whatever touch of inspiration I thought I had in writing it was gone. On referring to my script, I found a bit here, a bit there, this end of a scene, this key line of a scene changed or left out. Somebody had been there while I was gone. I discussed the matter some days later with another writer—a man who formerly had been a pretty well known but struggling novelist and now was an ace scenario writer with at least one Rolls-Royce and a seaplane to his credit. "Yes," he said, "they gave your script to me to look over. I hope you didn't mind. We often have to do that."

"Do what?" I asked.

"Well, smooth things up. You see, your script leaned

too much toward one of these cussed artistic productions, and that's a thing no studio will allow. There's not a cent of money in them."

"How do you know there's not?"

"Listen, this is a business out here, not an art. You'd better go back to Greenwich Village or South Carolina."

"North Carolina," I corrected with some heat.

"Well, wherever it is."

"But Chaplin"—I began.

"Yes, Chaplin!" he snapped.

"And Disney."

"Yes, Disney," he murmured.

4

My friend was right, as I well found out. Making pictures in Hollywood is a business, an industry, and with its present aims and methods has to be. This simple and first fact is the source of all the trouble that befalls anyone interested in the art of the cinema, whether he be actor, writer, musician, architect, dancer, sculptor, painter, or stage designer. Since the old nickelodeon days when this novel form of mass entertainment tapped a mine of riches for any hustling Tom, Dick, or Abie, money-making has been its prime aim. And this being true, it was logical that as the different studios developed they should follow the methods of big business and in the competitive market force a speeding up and leveling out of production that would prohibit any sort of experimentation or excursions into new creations. The only experimentation they can or will afford to be interested in is that of novelty. Let any new trick or gadget be invented which might be used to intrigue the populace through the till, and the executive will grab it in an instant. But let an Eisenstein or Rene Clair try to interest them in cinematic art and they politely but firmly refuse to hear. "We'd like to do fine things," they will always tell you, "but such pictures never pay. We'll show you the books."

The studios have a product to sell to the masses of the world, and in order to sell to everybody they think they must strike a common denominator of general illiteracy and bad taste. Perhaps they must. Their pictures are standardized by what they consider to be the intelligence quotient of the majority of people in the small villages and crossroad places. For there are many times more 14-year-old minds in the world than 20-year-old minds—and a dime is a dime no matter whose it is, and the best picture from the Hollywood point of view is the picture that attracts the most dimes. This is obvious and well known to everybody, but I mention it in order to somewhat explain, for instance, that pernicious institution known as censorship. That powerful organization is in actuality no other than a liaison body between the studios and the public. Outwardly it has as its intent the welfare of the country's morals. But what the organization really does is to keep the studios informed as to the varying whims of the 14-year-old mind and what is likely to go best in Ohio and not to go in North Carolina or vice versa.

By censoring each script carefully and reporting its findings to its employer (the producer), the censorship board saves the studios hundreds of thousands of dollars a year in wasted footage. No wonder the producers are willing to provide the salaries of that body, for after all it is one of the best paying parts of their business. And so it is that the writer who strives to create a script which in some way shall express the drama of his characters, or the problems of life as he feels them, is again and again defeated in his purpose by the censor. And once the censor says nay to a line or a scene, the writer is helpless. The producer simply has to point to the ruling of that office, if he cares to, and say, "Here's the public board on morality and customs. It says no"—and no it is. Sometimes a producer will overrule the censor, as in the case of a recent sensational convict picture, but these differences of judgment are rare.

Such difficulties as these, to repeat, make it impossible for one interested in the moving pictures as an art to sink himself in Hollywood without some loss in time, energy, and life's enthusiasm. He can replenish his purse perhaps, but it is likely to prove a costly gain otherwise. There is hardly any place on the globe so full of unhappy would-be artists—writers, musicians, actors, and poets. They are surfeited with hush money, but many of them cannot hush the gnawing that wakes them up at night when they think of the book they had planned to write, the play they yet will write, or the symphony that struggles somewhere within them. They are wearied to distraction trying to provide cheap stuff for actresses who know how to work for the public, and likewise for their illiterate consorts, the actors who know little more. And why should they not be wearied, yes, wearied and undone? For what joy, what encouragement and inspiration can there be in continuing to assist at the corruption and pollution of a people's soul?

5

But even so, Hollywood is essentially no worse than the old Broadway theatre, or for that matter the professional entertainment theatre in any great metropolis, a generation ago. In fact it is the old theatre in a new form. The movies through the universality of their medium have been able to provide more entertainment to more people at less cost than the old professional theatre could, and the Erlangers and Shuberts have pretty much disappeared. And just as the art or imaginative theatre grew out of a revolt against the professional theatre, so will the art or imaginative cinema grow out of the professional movies. The hundreds of dissatisfied creative minds, whose sole job day after day is the making of money for bankers, millionaires, and stockholders, will some day—and very soon at that—break into open revolt. There is no price large enough to keep a rebellious spirit indefinitely enslaved. Already a few independent producers, writers, and artists are trying a few forlorn experiments in creating pure forms of cinematic art, both here and abroad. And just as the imaginative theatre has had its Appia, its Stanislavsky, and its Craig, so will the new imaginative cinema have its apostles and philosophers who, following the lead of Charlie Chaplin and Disney, will give to the art a statement of new form and vital method. And when this new art has broken itself loose from the industry and professionalism of Hollywood and started on its own path, we shall see moving picture dramas worthy of the name. Writers, actors, directors, and musicians will then take joy and pride in their work and will strive to the best of their minds and souls to deal with the camera as its essential nature provides. And what they create will be of their own making, and the writers will be free to write scenarios as full of imagination and poetry as their gifts will allow. And these scenarios will have the dignity of publication, just as the stage plays are now published, and the author will have every privilege in the art cinema that his brother playwright has in the art theatre.

6

In the imaginative cinema, as I like to call it, which is soon to be a power in the world, this truth will be recognized; namely, that the art of the cinema is not the art of the theatre. And conversely the theatre—(that is, the imaginative theatre, for no other is really left, now that the movies have taken over the professional theatre)—this theatre must realize that its art is not that of the cinema. Each has a nature of its own, and each must interpret man and his world in its own technique. But in each the poet as a creator shall be supreme. In the cinema he has a means of universal and infinite power—the camera. In the theatre he likewise has a means of universal and infinite richness—the intimate presence. In the former he has an invention which eradicates all the material difficulties of depiction which beset the stage, but which projects forth only shadows of two dimensions and begins with a certain aloofness therefor. In the latter he has the embodied being which projects only itself and in three dimensions and begins with a complete and vital closeness therefor. And as the essential nature of the camera is expressed in panto-mime and accompanying sound, so the essential nature of the intimate presence is expressed in words and accompanying pantomime.

And in this new cinematic art form we shall some day find the complete expression of genius. And that genius we await. Chaplin is the forerunner of some cinema Shakespeare-to-be. As yet there is no forerunner in the imaginative theatre for the coming apostle of the shining word. But the growing concerted effort of people believing and working in the art theatre throughout the world is providing the way. And soon, very soon, we shall have on the one hand the art cinema with its triumphant beauty and on the other hand the art theatre with its triumphant beauty; and what the latter may lack in flexible distribution it will make up for in intensity.

Now those who lament the death of the theatre before the onslaught of the movies do not grasp the essential differences of the two mediums and likewise forget the godlike power which resides in the word spoken by the intimate presence. It is immortal and cannot die, and a theatre founded on it will never perish. The theatre is not dead. Only the worst of it is dead or moved elsewhere. Let that worst go with its methods of industry and mass marketing. The best, more purified and certain of itself shall stand, for the very essence of time and the nature of man is that before history is finished the best shall somehow come forth to light.

But this theatre of the imaginative word and intimate presence must refit itself more in terms of the machine age if it is to be free and powerful as it should be. It must take a lesson from the flexibility and universality of the camera medium and make more, flexible and universal its own medium. It must throw away the bothersome clogs of too many material props which impede the flow and lift of the dramatist's story. Slight suggestions and symbols should be sufficient. Let the poet follow his story wherever it leads—into bogs, boudoirs, or skyscrapers. Let the word speak. With the great advance in discoveries concerning light, almost any change of scenery and scene effect can be worked instantaneously; and when the curtain goes up on the stage the processes of fade-ins, fade-outs, and dissolves which the movies have discovered can be used so that the dramatist's imagination and the audience's attention remain one.

7

And under such conditions poetry will return again to the stage, and the freedom that Shakespeare knew in his Elizabethan theatre will be ours with greater enchantment. And whereas the new cinema art form will be the imaginative sight and sound unlimited, so the new theatre will be the home of the imaginative word and vitalized being unbound. And once more, as in the days of Shakespeare, we shall be able to parade before our vision all the manifestations of nature and the subtleties of the mind which are usable in the movie medium. And once more music in the theatre will return to us, above which the high poet's words are calling. And perhaps as never before the earth with its trees and flowers, the skies with their storms, the darkness of the night, the fear of wandering spirits, the hates, the passions and grandeur and omnipotence of God himself shall be evoked and spoken forth.

This the stage should do.

This the camera will do!

Art and Religion

ART LIKE RELIGION IS UNIVERSAL AND INFINITE, AND every man shares in it according to his ability and desires. This is true of the smallest man and the proudest, the best and the worst. In appreciation all men are artists more or less, and in the creation of beauty the same is true. But some men possess such desires and abilities to a greater degree, and these are generally given the name artists; whereas those of weaker sensibilities and gifts are usually understood to be outside that category. The artist as such is one who by the skillful use of symbols transmits his feelings, ideas, and visions to others in such a way that their appreciation of themselves and the world is heightened.

Discrimination of values is necessary in judging the art object and likewise the artist. By agreement of tradition and individual testimony some creations of artistic genius are greater than others. Therefore even in the universality of the subject matter and its applicability the man of judgment must distinguish the better from the worse, the higher from the lower. And at once we are led into the age-old problem of morality and art. But this is a difficulty to be solved, not a discouraging answer to be accepted, and in simple words the answer is—that the higher the art the more it ennobles, the lower the more it degrades. Apart from aesthetic history, most of us know the truth of this contention by our own experiences. Barbaric and voluptuous music, blatant military bands, a clamorous ritual of the evangelist often achieve an immediate and disastrous effect by drowning all judgment and common sense, so that the participant is a prey to the cheap mood and meaning of the occasion. On the contrary an Aeschylean tragedy, a symphony of Beethoven, the heroic figures of Michelangelo may serve to exalt us and at the same time stir our powers of feeling and reason to a more complete unity of vision and purpose. By common consent of statistical philosophy, proofs in endless number could be adduced concerning the moral and immoral power of art. But no amount of mathematics can help us in deciding what we need to feed our spirits upon. The ancient commandment of adhering to the good and growing away from the bad is generally good enough for our purpose.

But how shall one specifically distinguish between the good and the bad in art? This is a metaphysical question to most of us and is usually put away from consideration by a typical and gentle answer that "if I like a thing it is good, if I dislike it it is bad—for me." This individual and democratic judgment is an old story and an easy escape for one not bothered over-much with either curiosity or the cat. If X says that the "St. Louis Blues" is a fine piece of music simply because he likes it, he is in the main making a subjective and quantitative valuation. If another person says he dislikes this composition and thinks it bad because it outrages his feelings—he too is guilty of the same sort of judgment.

Though these views are not entirely false, they err in being piecemeal and partial. The old I-like-it or I-like-it-not philosophy of a George Jean Nathan, say, is not sufficient if one would continue the stretches of his reason for longer than a mood, a moment, or a day. For suppose that X, who likes the "St. Louis Blues," is a man of naïve emotions whose judgment is simple and untrained, who has experienced little in what men have agreed upon as civilization, culture; and suppose that the second person, say, is a Brahms—then the chances are that the judgment of the second person is nearer the truth we are seeking than that of the first—though often X the peasant may discern a kind of quantitative, a small and immediate beauty which the sophisticated, the wider-ranged man will miss.

However, the fact that the subject falls into this double question of good and bad proves that a subjective judgment is not sufficient in itself, and that the judgment of the judger is to be considered in weighing the validity of his conclusions. In other words, in distinguishing the better art from the worse we must decide between the better appreciator and the worse, and to do so leads us to the necessary conclusion that there is an objective standard in aesthetic considerations as well as a subjective one. Now the objective and subjective phases of the matter are not antagonistic; in fact they become one in the complete aesthetic experience.

Consequently in judging a better or worse work of art

we must inquire as to its effect upon ourselves both in terms of ourselves and the external world, and likewise we must so value the creator himself. This returns us to the definition given in the first paragraph. To repeat, we must consider what the work of art, the play, the moving picture, the novel, the symphony makes us feel and think about our world, ourselves, and about our fellowman. In an immediate aesthetic experience these questions do not always obtrude themselves, but they necessarily follow upon that experience, contemplatively follow if it is valid and real. In an honest search of ourselves we will find the old truth—that a good or noble work of art heightens our pleasure in and adherence to the Good; that is, each one under its spell re-affirms in himself the desire and finer purpose of his life and stands ever stronger in the gripping certainty of an absolute reality and meaning to his existence and that of others like him. In this, art and religion are one and stand opposed to the pessimisms of a specialized science.

Southern Commonwealth:
A Case In Point

1

I T IS RECORDED IN THE BIBLE THAT JESUS ONCE CAME upon some fellows lamenting the lack of anything doing. "Cast down your nets where you are," He said. And they did. We know what happened. This is the sort of parable that fits many things, not the least of all the lack and dullness of my State in any form of art, a condition lamented by the new patriots now for many a year. But the lamentations have been in the voice of the Pharisee. They have not been in earnest. Nobody has cried aloud and wept that he was undone.

From its beginning, three hundred years ago, until the present, North Carolina has made no lasting contribution to the culture of the world. Several millions of people have lived and died there, and no one has set himself aside in high-minded and intelligent devotion to record a single one of these lives, or to propound in the devious ways of the artist's craft any of the hopes, struggles, disappointments and attainments that made up the sum of their existence. And from knowledge of the past it would seem that such a record is worth while.

This state has never produced a single great work of art. I am not talking about the factories, railroads, agricultural and commercial industries, and the many and one creations of what is more or less called the practical mind. In a way they are forms of art too. At least they have their aesthetic side—their pattern, their fulfilled design and completed function and, in addition, the pleasure of the maker and planner. But one must remember that they also have produced their slaves. What I am especially concerned with here is the so-called finer arts. And as far as they count we can call the hogs till our tongues drop out and there will be no stir in the pasture.

Have we had a great painter? A great musician? A great sculptor? A great architect? A great poet, novelist, essayist, biographer—a great anything so far as the subject of art is concerned? We have not. We've not had even an adequate one in any of these. Other states in the union, to limit the matter, have had their Emerson, Longfellow, Thoreau, Poe, Whitman, Mark Twain, Henry Adams, Whistler, St. Gaudens, Winslow Homer, Henry James, Stanford White, Theodore Dreiser, Edith Wharton, Willa Cather, Elizabeth Madox Roberts, Edna Millay, Sinclair Lewis, Robinson Jeffers, Upton Sinclair, Eugene O'Neill, Grant Wood, William Faulkner, Thomas Benton, John Steinbeck, and many others. I mention these simply at random. But we North Carolinians have had no one. The two born here who really mattered—O. Henry and Thomas Wolfe—had to flee their home to find their souls

elsewhere and give them voice. They felt suffocation and
perishment coming on.

2

And how explain this lack, this dullness of the records
of our lives and days? For it is true that we have had
plenty of records, plenty of thus and so, and about it and
about, but nothing great and real, nothing first-rately en-
lightened or enlightening. We've had numerous local
crossroad poets, would-be novelists, columnists, dabblers
in water colors, and bangers on musical instruments. None
of them have had much meaning for you and me, nor for
the world at large. We haven't bred the real thing. And
why? Nobody knows. There are a thousand and one
possible prognostics and theories, but they are no more
than partial descriptions and come long after the train's
done gone.

There was no explanation as to why those fellows in the
parable were in the midst of dull business except the
simple one that they were not fishing. And the only answer
to our lack and dullness is the likewise simple one that we
haven't been at the business of production. Then how can
we produce art? Nobody knows. Why we haven't done it
and how may we do it—both are mysteries. It all is part
of that strange matter known as living. As the Scriptures
put it, and as Hamlet put it, "It will come when it will
come." But be it ever so mysterious, we don't profit by
laying the burden on God or on the weather. There are
aids—some in the form of prayers and some in the form
of everyday matters. They are only aids though, and can
never be more. The cause and source will forever be mys-

terious, and so discussion is pretty much worthless *except* as it concerns these aids and the individual who strives to use them.

3

One of the first and most apparent helps towards an escape from this artistic lethargy and emptiness is to become acutely conscious that such is our condition. That is relatively an easy matter. We only have to look at the facts. They are written down in the records and an eyeless man running can read them. As soon as we know what we are and have been so long, it is unthinkable that we shan't try to improve. The second and realest help is the most difficult and yet the most necessary, if we are to do our duty before God and man—the duty of building monuments in the name of what is finest and most beautiful in the lives of human beings around us. And that also is a becoming conscious. It is the becoming conscious of the marvel of being alive. It is not a moral matter, nor a practical matter. It rather is more nearly that something symbolized and denoted in the word *spiritual*—the word that had significance for souls in Victorian days and of late again in a breaking world is finding use and meaning. Now how can we so become conscious? If it were as difficult as it seems at first sight, certain and many of us would be condemned to hell from the beginning. But it so happens that here there is no dogmatic division of sheep and goats, of lost and saved in this province. For all people (even idiots, maybe) have this consciousness, this sense of beauty, to be specific. But they have it more or less. And the whole burden and responsibility rests upon our making the less more.

And how can that be done? How can there be progress towards such a coming to pass? There is no definite answer, for it is essentially individual with every individual. In the main he must work it out for himself. The institutions of education, the technologies of industries that minister to man's comfort cannot give it, cannot of themselves increase it. They can but be used as partial means in this process. Again, it is a personal matter of a man's own living. He has the privilege of choice from books, he can draw from wind and weather, from inspiring lives about him, from the broken and the oppressed, from the triumphant and successful—from all that walk on God's green earth and under God's high heaven. He can draw sustenance from all that is around him. He can increase within him more and more the light that lighteth. And for all men there is this strange way of salvation, and no one can save him but himself. So cast down your nets where you are if you dwell by the sea. Or if a laborer in the field, go forth with strength and song. Push on, let heads be raised and faces set to the rising sun. In the cool of the evening God will walk there and a blessing will remain on the lifted or the bowed.

At least it seems so.

4

And so I for one hold that all this burst of recent writing and talk in the state—this work, for instance, in folk plays, the putting out of new magazines, the writing of more books, the founding of dramatic clubs, study groups, clubs and more clubs, discussion and re-discussion—all are good. These are working along with, and in a sound way are supplementing, the schools and colleges; they are gradually making literature and other forms of art things of concern with us generally and are serving to help us get our eyes open. And don't we need it? We need to stir our will-power, revivify our senses, shake our minds out of their deadness. Rise and shine, as the Negroes sing. And the more we shine the more power we have to shine— that's our blessed miracle, even as the ever-renewing radiance of the sun. And that alone so far as I can see is our proper excuse for being. If that is true—and it is true —the Bible and the Victorians still have much worthy our study and appreciation. Go to it—all is part of our world, and the world is for our appreciation, or it remains wasted upon us. In the words of a revised version, grow in grace. So will it to be and struggle to bring it to pass, and our heavy responsibility is somewhat discharged. Then upon a day iron palings that divide will be less cruel and the chanted convict song will change from a dark lament in bondage to a ring-shout in freedom. I believe that. And the fear of the low for the powerful will be lessened. The slave will see some easement in his chains, and the pitiful and lost will have the records of their lives set down. And they the more will not have lived in vain. For it is by such living records, records and more records, that we can pack up, store up and hand down accumulated living unto those that come after, and they thereby shall be made more aware of the power and glory of man and the universe in which he struggled for a season. They will have more food to feed upon, more possibilities of quickening their lives to wonder and joy.

5

And what material we have had and put to no use!—
material for music, drama, poems, pictures, novels, songs
—matter for dreams. But we've had no dreamers. Where
is the man, where are the men? Come out of your hiding-
place. Strike up the harps, let the bands play. Where shall
we find him who will light up the struggles of our people?
Who will tell of the builders, the road-makers, the pioneers, the creators of cities, or railroads? Their records
stand unsupported in themselves. Let them have their
place in story and song—in the illumination of art. Are
these high-sounding phrases? They have some meaning.
Who among us has told the story of the lonesome seashore,
of the early settlers along that ocean, of the wrecks and
disasters there? Nobody. Along the empty sand banks lie
the rotting ribs of many a ship, the disappearing records
of struggle and death. In that wide and barren land of
sand and battered trees are symbols of man and his
bravery enough to move an army. And yet through all
these years they have failed to touch the heart of a single
North Carolinian, I mean touch him so that he has had to
cry out in the exquisite pain of creativeness. And the light
and darkness among those sounds and shallows there, and
the wonders in the sky above! Where is our painter? He
is not yet born, or he is away from home. Maybe he is at
a metropolitan cocktail party talking of essences and
purity of significant form. Ride among the sand-hills in
the evening. Who has painted a sunset in Moore County?
Nobody. Walter Hines Page came home from the court of
St. James to see it all before he died. He cared enough for
that. Who else will care and make it his business to speak

to the brethren in the valley? Little men, big men, where
are you hiding? ...Who has sung of our mountains?
Spring or autumn, they cry for a voice. One Wordsworth
among them would carry inspiration to millions before the
curtain came down. Who tells the romance of the farmer's
life among his tobacco, his cotton and corn? Nobody.
And the mighty Negro and his life that was and is to be—
there as he spills his song, laying the great mudsills,
slinging his pick, digging out the canals, smoothing the
roads, he the rider of dreams? I hear no answer. Or the
great winter migration of the tenant John Smith and his
family in search of a better home over there in Sampson
or up in Harnett or down in Pender Counties? Call the
roll of the chosen ones. Who recounts the drama of the
country doctor and his fight against ignorance and poverty,
flies and dysentery and typhoid fever—his devotion to
the needy in freeze and flood? Who has told his story?
Nobody. And the matters of statecraft and politics, an
epic tale of wisdom and gentleness, of cunning and graft,
of bribery and dealings at the pie-counter? Where is our
Balzac or Tolstoi or Chekhov? Asleep or gone on a journey. The dinner-bell rings, the house burns down, but no
one comes. .... Yes, yes, everywhere round us, both here
and yonder, is work for willing hands to do, hands that
will shape and build to the finer uses of a living art.

And the hands will some day be reached forth. I believe
that, I hope that. And in such a day we shall be happier
and worth more to ourselves and to all others. So, if I may,
I would call to the younger ones. For the old have long ago
sold their goods and moved into Babylon. And the younger
ones will answer, are answering. I hear them. I see them.

The Playwright In Revolt

1

THE PLAYWRIGHT, LIKE OTHER ARTISTS, IS ALWAYS in revolt, that is more or less. Not only is this true of artists, but likewise of people and things.

The word is a difficult one, and if a metaphysic for it were sought it could be found in the old dualism of changing permanence stated in Greece some twenty-five hundred years ago and still a bafflement to the philosophers of this day.

It is the nature of that which exists—including the living and the dead—to make use of antagonisms and differences in the assertion of itself. In fact, such is the nature of that assertion.

Revolt then is but another term for development or growth—development which is contemporaneous in all existence, going on at any instant of time and in every part of space. In this sense all things are in continuous revolt, that is, all things are alive, with the constant qualification of more or less.

Thus any production is the production of something new from the old. Nor is this new ever the same as the old, for there can be no repetition either in nature, art or things, only similarity. In mechanics where the methodology might demand sameness there is constant wear and tear and response to varying taste and needs and inner upheavals; and there is no continuance in iteration.

The term development is more in keeping with a certain richer way of the world than revolt. The former means fulfillment of and the latter denial of. And it would appear that life absorbs denial in its growth in so far as life is spiritual—if one may use a word so heavily suspect. And one must use it for completeness' sake, and in these latter days for the soul's sake.

2

Since the present then is always in revolt or developing, it is in that consequence the best of all possible times. It could not be otherwise, for in its development it contains the past, the present, and the future, inasmuch as they are significant to us the living:—the past which has shaped us to the present, the past and the present upon which it feeds and acts, and the present and future which is its fruitfulness.

To repeat, this is truest of what might be called the spiritual nature of man and not of the process and wastage of physical nature and things. Accordingly the ancient statement that "now is the accepted time" is always true for man. Errors, mistakes, failures, and tragedies do not alter this, for negative and positive matters alike are one for him therein.

The recent preachment that the present is a time of cultural waste and decay has found widespread concurrence among the confused, the tired and discouraged who have been overpowered by the richness, variety, and upboilings of life and mistakenly apprehended these as antagonistic to art when in reality they are the food and inspiration of art.

Pessimism, therefore, is a partiality, and at any real moment of experience there is no cause for it. The weak keepers may tremble, but the light suffers no diminution, it ever increases. And Everyman ever grows stronger in his service to it. He neither revolts nor despairs, nor has ears for the phrases coming out of the distance that all is hopeless. These are ejaculations of hurt cast up in the heat of battle by the weak of arm and frail of will who fall afoul of themselves in the darkness near the edge of light.

And by that light Everyman writes in his book. He is the artist.

3

And as artist he is full of present great possibilities never before dreamed of and which he encompasses in his increasing wisdom.

With the canons of novelty and entertainment some would purvey him into their darkness, but confusion cannot dismay him nor can it deter him. For him beauty still walks upon the earth as in the days of Helen, or Eve, or any Thais. Nor is the whole story told therein, for he will have his say and speak his vision.

And as artist he is stronger and freer in the living present. Like the rumor of old he increases by continuing, grows great by what he feeds upon. And his food is the multitudinous and ever-outpouring matter of life itself which fertile nature in all her forms provides.

And his spirit is freer than before in this province which is the all—the all that exists, all that can be thought or experienced. Nothing for him is tabooed or set apart or closed off. All is native to his need. All that is mechanical, all that is vital with which the world is overflowing, all that has been created—these are his.

4

And as dramatist they are the inventions and the arts, the facts and things and deeds and events of life, to be combined and transformed with infinite variety into his dream made manifest—history, poetry, music, painting, dancing, sculpture, architecture, pantomime:—hills, streams, woods and all weather, the sciences and all knowledge, and all the machinery of the modern world.

And from these he is creating the great art, the great drama, which is his new religion, his new mystery and philosophy.

5

And in the process his two ancient enemies fall before him—morality which would bind him in its creeds, and commerce which would use him to its purpose, the former confusing beauty with ethical customs, the latter vision with gain. The artist knows no immoral art, no immoral drama. There can be bad art, bad drama. And morality with its censorship must give way to aesthetic taste and sensitivity, not to the enforcement of law.

For to consider fancifully, if art corrupts, it will corrupt the judges of its corruption, and therefore the judges should be protected, since if they are corrupted their judgment is false and they are no longer judges and keepers of the truth—and so on to absurdity. Law cannot in any way deal with the matter, nor statute. Only intelligence and vision can.

And if art, the drama, to consider once more, is beholden to gain, to commercial enterprises and rents, gambling and exchanges, whims and fancies of its upholders, it is no longer art but a symbol of barter and vanity, in which beauty becomes a figment on an expedient currency.

All these things the artist knows and will show to others in time and as he can.

6

And the dramatist writes the great drama for the theatre envisioned in this present. This theatre is the home of his art with schools and training grounds, rooms, laboratories, and workshops for experiment in mechanics and all the arts—for all these will coöperate in the drama as it appears complete upon the stage of its new home, a home consisting of a studio, an auditorium, an amphitheatre, and a large outdoor stadium, these four being the reason for all other buildings begot around them.

And this home of buildings is the great theatre—with its director, its playwrights, its actors, artists, artisans, and inventors—all parts of the greater whole, to which they give existence and from which they draw inspiration.

And this too will suffer revolt and develop into something new and different. Such is the creative mystery and glory of both our art and our life.

Democracy In Woeful Times

(A LETTER IN REPLY)

1

I WAS GLAD TO GET YOUR LETTER OF THIS WEEK AND sorry to hear that you had been under the weather, so to speak. I was sorry also to hear that you had just finished reading my last play and had hurled the book with an oath across the room. All vague and vacuous words, you say, something about an American dream. Well, now I hope with spring in full bloom and the dream-nighted January passed away, these mulligrubs which have infected you will be killed off by the warm light of summer and the "doleful doings" of your mind will give way to the persuasion of flowers and birds and trees and the rich profusion of life pouring out its sweet and everlasting miracle upon the land. That at least should help.

You say, in passing, you are fed up with your environment there—with its clang and clamor, its compressive turmoil of busy and failing lives, and wish you were out of it and back among the pines of Carolina. Frankly, John, I hear that sort of story often and remember my father's old saying about cows off yonder having long horns or the grass being greener in another pasture, old sayings that fitted your case the day you left us for your future there just as they maybe fit you now that you want to come back again. And as for the social ways of a lot of the people around you there, the baiters and the bunders, the manikins and minikins with their psyches and their dogs, the ism-fanatics, the birth-control professionalists, the cultural center aesthetes clasped emptily together for comfort and for art—to list but a few you mention—well, they are to be found everywhere and you won't escape them by coming here. For as both Brigham Young and Schopenhauer have well shown, along with Solomon, desire is mighty and will prevail, and all kinds of people are forever being dumped into this world. Activity continues, and when sex is off economics is on, and usually both are putting in full time together.

Yes, like a mighty tree, old life keeps pumping us up in sap from below to spill out as long as time shall last in rich fruitfulness at the top. If some of the twigs do freeze and die, the main and leafy wonder still goes on. And I wouldn't waste too much worry on these perverse and blighted twigs, either. They will rot and fall to the ground to add their pinch of fertilizer to the enrichment of the mystic bush above. This has always been true—as witness the million cold April-bud little poets, artizans, and inventors who have added their small mite to the big things that happen in the world. This is the process known and accepted in the Orient long before the western world was thought of, and we might do well to consider it. I refer you to the Hindu scriptures which can now be got in a cheap edition of Everyman's Library. Also Tagore's philosophical essays. You might draw some comfort from them. You know we used to talk a lot about these things when we were students there at the University. I have discovered the books since then.

2

Now, this all sounds a bit hardboiled and unsympathetic—like a kind of let-things-wag-as-they-will philosophy, and don't give a hang. I don't mean it that way. I believe that the burning bush or green tree of life—use what figure you will—is endowed with the miracle of consciousness, of emotion, mind and will—and all of us its parts have the power and the bounden duty to help it grow into the world as a thing of beauty forever. That is not only the opportunity and urge of man but his instinctive joy also. There are failings away all along the line of course like those you mention above and like those we see every day in any forest. And it has to be so because of an infinity of environmental and heredity factors which can never wholly be made to behave. But the main body of the tree, of humanity, does not fail and never will, only the bitten twigs and sunless branches die. And when you cry out in your middle-aged distress along with H. G. Wells and others that all is confusion and despair in a world of strife and you would, please suh, rest from it and give over, I know you are wrong and hasten once more for my own clarification and your encouragement to tell you so. I have a sort of abdominal philosophy, an inner witness as it were, that testifies even in the small hours to me that the course of man is upward and not downward. For in the first place man wills it so and in the second it is the way all things in the large seem fated to proceed. It has taken me a long time to throw off the pessimism which our professors of rationalistic philosophy and science taught me as a student, and maybe if you thought around a while you would find some of their old wayward words still whispering to you from the "subconscious" dark.

In these latter days, to repeat, I have found a deeper wisdom than theirs among the Hindus, in certain of the New Testament scriptures such as the first chapter of *John* and the seventh chapter of *Romans,* and in Greek philosophers like Plato, Parmenides, Heraclitus, and Plotinus. All of these feel, know, and affirm a righteous logic in the universe, a logos, a principle of goodness which nothing can destroy for man except man himself, and he will not do it because he cannot prevail upon himself to so deny himself. In particular and perverted cases, yes, but never in the main and vital body of the tree of humanity. Do not all men of whatever creed or calling as a rule appeal to this goodness? It is their light, the guide by which they act and do their business. Their ways of finding it are different, and in this difference they often mistake the lesser good for the greater, and as a consequence wars and killings and grievous things continue to happen among us. But these too will pass away—in a long time, a long, long time. Here the challenge is sharpest for our so-called educators and political leaders. Let them get busy and help to shorten that time and so save suffering, but not by graphs and tables and edicts from above. Oh, no! Only by the wisdom of an understanding and loving heart. How then, you say, can new hearts be given to these so diseased ones except by cutting out the old and inserting the new, and then the body dies? Apart from all cuttings, let that body die, as even Polonius himself would say. Thereafter we shall consider.

And then after deploring the condition of the world and your especial section of it, John, you say in your letter that you are wretched over the breakdown of American ideals in these latter days. Nay, you go further and declare that these woeful times have proved too clearly that the American system of thought, its democracy, is an idle dream talked about a great deal but never proved, and now with the avalanche of totalitarianism rolling towards us we have nothing with which to meet the enemy, no real defense against him. Here in your letter you wax lyrical with pessimism and doubt. America has never done anything high and ideal in the history of the world, you say. We have always been a dog-eat-dog nation if the truth were acknowledged, and before we can get anywhere we've got to recognize ourselves for what we are—a selfish money-getting, sharp-trading land of usurers. We have no muscle, no stamina. Far better if we had a hard mailed fist at this doleful hour. Ah, and what have the foolish poets sung so long? you ask—"When in the course of human events—," "Certain inalienable rights—," "Government of the people, by the people, and for the people."

Words, words, you say. Yes, and yet more words, even my own, pleading as they will—

> Out of the rich and deep-bosomed earth,
> Mother of all, life-giving and bountiful,
> Thou builder and thou leveler,
> For thee these words.

Shall not the stones speak, the towering craggy trees
Watchfully waiting on the western hills—
The soft-reeded rivers, the valleys and the springs,
And all of man's making, the roads and the bridges,
Beams and girders and the reaching cables—
The walls and the towers, the fences and the wayfares—
Are these dead and voiceless things empty of meaning?

The scythe drops down, the hammer nerveless drops,
The plow and the shovel wait unused and still,
The weeds take them, the roots thread their
    sightless sockets through,
The handles shaped to human hands dissolve in dust,
And the fierce and clamorous strength that used
    them once,
That ditched and dug and builded with them there
Is gone forever in the tomb.
What then, shall their dreaming and their purpose
    all be lost,
The head of agony upon the pillow turned for naught?

Out of the tomb is there no voice now,
There by the low enclosing wall of quiet,
Silent in the evening's grievous hush?—
All is muted in the fresh upflaming morn,
All tongueless waits the lordly mountain top.
Shall these souls be bound in the tremulous
    chains of the starlight,
Or dust and ashes befoul the bright head of beauty—
O fading footsteps lost forever,
O eloquent lips, the passionate hearts,
And gesturing final hands!—
Shall these forever be as if they'd never been?

Nay, cry out the roll call of their prideful names,
Wake with the reveille of our buoyant song
These that lie forgotten and foregone.
Now all our walking is the paths they trod,
Our speech their same shaped mouth and tuneful tongue,

Our gestures still the same strong-fingered hand,
Plucking the bouquets, firing the guns,
Building and shaping and creating in their stead.
So thus the dead do live in us again,
And we the living honorably may die.

I believe that, John, and I'm sure you are wrong—not because you attack Jefferson, Lincoln, and any multitude of others, but because you attack the deep and human vision by which we claim to live. America has done great things and will do other great things, noble things. It's not all words. And what great things beyond the dollar and the dime? you ask with weary and doubting irony.

3

All right, then, the conquering of this vast wilderness of the western world. It was not an easy thing to do, but our forefathers did it—slowly step by step, ax blow by ax blow, and furrow by furrow. At first only the precarious hold upon the eastern fringes of this land was theirs. Then with incredible hardship and toil from father to son and to other sons they made their way inland, up into the hills, to the mountains, over the mountains, across the rivers and the plains to still other mountains north and south till another ocean three thousand miles away was reached. You know all these facts from your history books. And out of this wide and boundless struggle with nature a strong self-reliance was developed, untrammeled by any clan intrigues, fealties, and old-world loyalties of Europe. The mother country was far away, and day by day grew farther both in space and memory, and these her children, as is the course of things, came to be men in their own right and jealous of their hard-won prerogatives, feeling a proud ownership in the place and product of their toils. And as they depended on their skill, their industry and strength without appeal or favor from others, so did they grow to resent exploitation by any outside authority. It's true, as you in your present state of discouragement are quick to point out, these pioneers in conquering the wilderness did from the very abundance of the land and its resources set the habit of waste and carelessness which has come so evilly down to this day. We must remedy such mistakes and are doing it. Even here there is work to do instead of repining like the insect in the fable.

Then there followed the creation of the democratic ideal of government. Try as you will you can't laugh or sneer that off. For centuries men had dreamed of such an ideal, had written and preached about it—Confucius, Plato, Jesus, John Locke, and countless others—but none had ever found the proper statement for it or the time and place to put it into practice. And when on that long ago day of June 12, 1776, the Virginia House of Burgesses adopted the Bill of Rights as finally drawn up by the leading thinkers of that colony, something new had begun among men. I believe that. With this basic statement made, the Declaration of Independence and the Constitution of the United States soon were derived. Here at last and for the first time in the history of the world a system of government was begun, based upon the recognition of the absolute worth of the individual, which declared that each and every man is an ultimate reality in himself and as such has certain inalienable rights that go with being a man. Nothing shall take these rights away from him. And to protect him in these rights, and for this reason only, gov-

ernments can be said to rightfully exist. He shall be secure
in his person and the earnings of his hands and brain. No
one shall unjustly imprison him or visit excessive punish-
ment upon him. He shall be free to go and come as he
pleases, to speak his mind openly and freely, to think as
he pleases, and to worship his God as he sees fit.

These are self-evident principles, our forefathers said,
and irrespective of color, creed, or previous condition of
servitude, men everywhere instinctively know them as
true. For after all, men are individuals before everything
else. Is not their birth, their love, and their death their very
own and nobody else's? Can they feel with another's hands,
eat with another's mouth, or think with another's mind?
No, their very being is their own and theirs alone. Man is
who he is and nobody else. Can a child grow into manhood
lying in the arms of his father? Or a daughter be more
than that on the bosom of her mother? No, they must grow
up. In homely phrase, every tub must stand on its own
bottom.

Democracy is a philosophy fitted to men full grown,
men who acknowledge themselves as morally responsible
beings as well as free, and who accept the rights that go
with that responsibility. They accept freedom in terms of
responsibility and responsibility in terms of freedom.

4

And now the abuses. Yes, there are plenty of them. Our
vision still exceeds our accomplishments, our reach, our
grasp. But thank God we've had that vision, we've had the
reach, and day by day we are making progress towards
answering the challenge of those living words. And we

are doing it from these basic principles beneath, not blindly from above as is the case with too many governments known as totalitarian. Let us try to remember that.

And our pioneer leadership in the creation of this the machine age! For the first time in the history of the world this country has produced the ultimately perfect servant —call him the cotton gin, the gas engine, adding machine, electric motor, telephone, talking machine, radio, or what you will. And we have conceived of and created these machines for the service of the individual, the democratic man, as a means of lightening his toil, freeing him from economic slavery for exercises of things of beauty and the spirit and not for uses of hate and death and destruction. We so conceive of them and will as long as our democratic philosophy remains deeply integrated into the bone and blood-beat of our life as it is now.

Here again the vision is being abused. Too many of our leaders continue to be contaminated by the urge to profit and the main chance. But we must not despair. It takes time, a long, long time for the hypocrites, windbags, and blackguards to die. But ultimately they will, and will receive their fitting reward and epitaph. No system works perfectly, whatever the first reaches of its dream may proclaim, and the challenge always is towards a more and more perfect fulfillment.

To return to my former figure—this growing of the mystic tree into the nobility of full form is a long process. It cannot suddenly be flowered into the sky by any artificial propagation or stimulus. It has to grow from the deep roots below, and this a power-sprung Europe and Japan will learn when their crises are past. It is easy to fight wars, it is hard to dramatize peace. Democracy's business

is with the latter even when the militancy of marching feet
and gleaming bayonets is required.

5

No, John, I do not share your discouragement about our
country. I am more keenly alive to its greatness now than
ever before. All of this turmoil and trouble you speak of
had to come. It is the convulsion of a new order breaking
through the world. And that new order, when the convulsion is finished, will be one nearer democracy than otherwise. Don't scoff, for I am in earnest. It may be called by
some other name, but when it comes the individual must
have his rightful place in it, must be recognized for what
he is as a free soul with certain inalienable rights and
responsibilities, or else the convulsion will break out
again.

Humanity is on the march to freedom, not to slavery,
and nothing will stop it. The winning of the wilderness
here, the riving out of our constitution, the creation of the
machine age, are steps towards that world freedom, and as
we have been pioneers in the past so must we continue to
be in the future. And not until the new international order,
in which both individuals and nations have their rightful
place, has come to pass can we count the victory ours. And
we must strive to spare the blood, John, spare the blood
and the tears in that mighty undertaking.

And in that new day this country will begin the fourth
great adventure of its history—the adventure of culture.
Art, literature, music, philosophy, and true science will
flourish then as never before. We are ready for them, and

you be ready, too, John. Let us both add our sap to the main and leafy wonder, calling out with Whitman—

Give me, O God, to sing that thought,
Give me, give him or her I love this quenchless faith,
In thy ensemble, whatever else withheld withhold not from us
Belief in plan of thee enclosed in time and space,
Health, peace, salvation universal.

And herewith, John, I send you another play of American history, a sort of call to the highlands ahead. You may throw it across the room in disgust like the other one, but in doing so you can only criticize me and not the rightness of the thing I am trying to tell about. Nor will you in any whit diminish the joy I have had in constructing the story and bringing back to life these characters of the long ago —with something of their faith, their vision, and their cheerful song. Bear with me and read it through if you can.

So farewell, and send me a copy of your new book when it comes out. Don't forget the Hindu scriptures.

Music In the Theatre

1

SUNK INTO MY EARLIEST REMEMBRANCE AS A CHILD were the folk-dance, folk-song, the ballad, the mammy lullaby, the instrument—the fiddle, the banjo, the harmonica, the knocking bones, and country church organ. They were as native and integral to the life of the people among whom I lived as the Bible, the hymnbook, the hoe, the rake, the plough, the axe and blade which fitted so snugly to their heart and hand. When finally at the assumed age of accountability I tried to write plays and see them set upon the local stage, these musical expressions of voice and instrument kept pushing themselves up in humps and rivulets of song as a clamorous part of the material with which I had to deal. There was no escaping them. Everywhere and like the subterranean energy of a mole they left their tracery in my tended plans.

Later when I began to lift my vision and intent beyond the fence that shut in my father's farm and the life I knew to a wider world where boundless things were done and mighty men with mighty heads walked closer to the stars, I found this same aptitude of song and rhythmic urge present among them also as with the humble man. A song there was in every heart, suppress it how they would. All were poets, such as they were. All dreamed dreams no matter what they did or how uneasy lay their heads.

And in that wider world was music sounding through the town. Now perhaps it was the imagined echo of Drake's drum heard dimly down the corridors of time where other patriots and reckless men once marched. Again a multitude of crooners luring and soft at evening-time speaking of love and women sweet as sugar lumps. Or again the fierce hot clangor wrangle of harmony gorging up a dream of steel and stone from the entrails of the earth. Or still again the multitudinous tongues of little machines that bleated and warbled the beauty and wonder of the world's wares and merchandise—hairpins, mineral water, tobacco, soap, slippers, pipes, parlor lamps, shoes, and chewing gum. And finding a song on every lip, a melody in every heart, a wayward foot to every dance, I wondered to think that those who make the plays of men and what they do should so continue the pale cold page and set their characters down in dry cacophonous wordiness.

I would do it differently and write of what was there. And as I expected, when I tried to write about these mightier men there rose up in the pattern of the piece the same sharp hump and clamor of song and music that had cried its place in other scenes in other days. And I was glad to find it true, for so old life and memoried logic ran according to their form, and all was clear to my sense. But something in my efforts beat against the pricks. The cur-

tain fell, the order came, the scenery van was at the door.
Not once but twice, three times it happened so. And all was
as it was, no ripple, murmur, nothing to tell that I had been.
The old business was back at the old stand, doing well.
Zwei herzen und ein schlag. Mighty is love, it harmeth not,
all by a common process warmed and incubated.

Now maybe it was time to take a little stock—to draw
back in order to leap further, as the French are known to
do in other and kindred things. Into hiding with my books
I went and fell afoul of the theatre saga once more. The
Greeks came first, they always do, even beyond the
Chinese, Hindu, and Japanese—those hairy westerners
with their vision of the god-man fatefully doomed. And in
and out and round about, the Attic play played forth itself not only with words that told a story but with the flute,
the chorus song, the mask and dance that amplified and
intrenched their full effect.

Then next it was the medievalists with their god and
devil entangled in a ritual of salvation for man, and everywhere I found the sound of the choir, the priest intoning,
the rhythmic censer swung and organ blowing. And up to
shelter and cherish it all the great cathedral grew..

Next it was the Elizabethans shouting man's glory and
self-sufficiency in a dewy morning world, sailing as it were
to sea on a swollen river of images and words. And there
too was the sound of the song on every lip, the melody in
every heart and moving foot, the flourish of the trumpets,
the recorders, the hautboys, the viol, and the lute—all
playing down the sliding stream. And when they had gone
on by before my wandering gaze, nothing was left but a
vast silence now known to school children as the Restora-

tion age. Nothing was to break that silence but the wise-crack of the wit, the dry argument of the preacher, and a bit of bawdiness on the side. The years passed on with music hushed, lightened only once perhaps by Gay's minor talent in the ballad opera. And so it was.

But the long moons before birth turn in silence with life's increase. At last out of the sea into which the Eliza-bethans had disappeared there came leviathan bellowing up with all the sea-horns including his own blowing forth an announcement that sent the smaller fry flying up to die in the freezing woods before him. And for awhile the leap-ing legend ran that in Wagner the miracle was complete. Here was the ideal theatre dreamed about—here was the *summa theologica* which the Greeks could never write nor ritualize, which the medievalists failed at, and the Eliza-bethans missed as they warbled their native woodnotes wild, clear eyed but dreaming.

Now it is well known that a little man with the underhold can give his God a mighty big tussle, and for those who claim too much, who climb too high, the knives of those same little men can cut them down. Or if failing that, the gimlets of their reason will bore the big boys through and let the light shine in upon their inner workings. So it hap-pened to Wagner's claims. The little composers and musi-cologists, for instance, got hold of him and "seized" and chipped away his defense, but only his defense, for his music remained above their attack. Still they proved with their pricking pens and knives and gimlets that there were defective flaws in the body of his contention. And today the reading yodeler knows it's so. Wagner strove to unite drama and music as one, but his musical genius was supe-

rior to his dramatic talent and the word was swallowed by
the reverberant note. But his operas still remain great
operas and maybe always will.

After Wagner the Teutonic spirit, still pushing forward, split and carried the theatre in two directions. On
the one hand Ibsen with his outward but intense moralistic
argument, and on the other Strindberg with his moody
and musical psychologues of the inner man. Ibsen's
theatre ended with himself. Somewhat like Haydn he was
his own cocoon, his personal cul-de-sac. No disciple could
go beyond him except to land stuffed in that cul-de-sac.
A thousand could go beyond Strindberg and to freedom,
for in him a job was not finished but suggestively begun.
With him the modern theatre received a fresh impulse
and inspiration.

2

Some years ago I met Alexis Granowski, the great
Russian director. He had just brought his Jewish Moscow
State Theatre troupe from that city for a short season in
the German capital. The night before our meeting I had
seen one of his productions and was so taken by it that I
got a theatre friend to introduce me to him. He listened
with evident appreciation to my enthusiastic outbursts
over the kind of musical theatre which he had created.
"Yes," he said in thoughtful English, "I think the music
drama or musical play offers greater opportunity than
any other. I have been working in this kind of drama now
for ten years and every day convinces me of it. For instance, the use of musicalized pantomime, speech, and
facial expression can liberate all those imaginative over-
tones of human psychology which straight realism can

never touch. Also by the use of music all sorts of conventions and needs which otherwise might obstruct and disintegrate a production to nothingness can be got around—short cuts in scenery, properties, and staging methods can be obtained. Further, it is easier to go straight to the heart of your story, to reach its inner expressive symbolism, and most vital meaning. You say you liked my production of *Two Hundred Thousand?*"

"I certainly did. And tonight I'm going to see your *Travels of Benjamin the Third.*"

"Yes. It is the same style as the *Two Hundred.* In fact, as I said, all of our repertory is music drama. Have you anything like it in America?"

"No, we haven't."

"If I should ever be forced to leave Russia, America is the country I would go to to begin my theatre over again. Of all the nations of all the world America seems to me the richest in dramatic subject matter—conflicts of individuals, of types, of institutions and organizations—a land of boundless energy, color, music, imagination—in short, the most creative nation on the globe. I know something of your theatrical history—I have heard of a few of your pioneer workers like William Vaughan Moody, Percy Mackaye, and of recent years of Eugene O'Neill. Who else have you?"

"We have Maxwell Anderson in the poetic drama. He is beating down a path, many of us feel, which will lead towards a new expression of American genius. And there are Sidney Howard, Robert Sherwood, Phillip Barry, Marc Connelly, Elmer Rice—"

"Do any of them make a great use of music?"

"I'm afraid not."

"Do you?"

"In a small way I have tried. To me it is the most inspiring kind of theatre."

"No doubt of that," he reiterated. "And why America hasn't developed music drama—" throwing out his hands —"well, that is one of these mysteries of art. But I prophesy before the real genius of your country can express itself on the stage, music vitally integrated into the drama itself must be used. For instance, why hasn't America ever created a great Negro theatre? More than once, in recent days and under the present regime (Russian) I have seriously considered moving to America to try to help build a Negro musical drama. Think of the rich possibilities you have there—the singing, the spiritual, the vivid religious ideology, folklore, the tall tales, the dramatic conditions surrounding that submerged yet marvelously gifted people."

"Some experiments are being made," I replied, "in Harlem, in Cleveland, Ohio, in Chicago, and in some of the larger cities. But they are only small experiments and nothing big yet has been done."

"Do you know Mr. Otto Kahn?"

"I've met him."

"He is here in Berlin now, and I was talking to him the other day about such an idea, and he offered to consider subsidizing a Negro theatre if I would come to America to head it. Well, it's a thing to think about."

I saw Alexis Granowski once or twice more. I was present at a meeting with him and a few others on the tragic night he reported that his theatre was dissolved by a command of the Soviet authorities. He remained in Berlin for a while, then moved to Paris where he later died. I never knew why he didn't come to America in accordance with this dream he had.

It has been more than ten years since that meeting. Mr. Kahn has also since died. Many American plays have been born and knocked their way on to the storehouse. Several Negro theatrical groups have been organized and dissipated. Dozens of musical shows have been written, made their money, received a redressing via Hollywood, amused the public, and passed on without remembrance. And the American music drama seems only a little nearer an actuality than before. But that little is encouraging. For there is a growing feeling on the part of American playwrights that such a drama needs to be. And in some of the productions like *The Green Pastures, Knickerbocker Holiday, Porgy and Bess,* and lately *Lady in the Dark,* and especially on the wide front of radio drama, progress is being made. And, too, in the great American people's theatre outside of Broadway (the real American theatre now) more and more attention is being paid to the use of music in plays. And someday not too far off the complete, vital use of the musical drenched word, rhythmic acting, and poetic speech no doubt will find embodiment and statement for a fervent audience.

I once heard Eugene O'Neill say, in reference to *Lazarus Laughed,* that the theatre would become a powerful force in American life only when some method was hit upon whereby the audience could participate in the performance somewhat as a congregation does in the ritual and service of the church. Whether this is true or not in sweeping generality is questionable. But if one remembers the power of music in religion and what religion would be without that music, is it not likely that a people's drama without music just so is lacking one of its most powerful and vitalizing elements? Yes.

The Artist In Time of War

(A LETTER IN REPLY)

I APPRECIATE YOUR FRANK AND STRAIGHTFORWARD letter as always, and I wish I could agree with your attitude about the war. But I can't, not now in these latter bitter days. And since you say as a friend you hope I will approve your stand, I will try to be as frank and straightforward as you have been in telling you why I cannot. Now believe me, I do it humbly enough and without any urge of seeming to be the source of wisdom to one less wise. I can only give you some of the conclusions I have arrived at after long pondering upon this present world of exploding fact wherein our dreams are being torn to tatters, yours and mine.

War is and always has been the great tragedy of man, specifically and generally. It is an experiment and experience in ultimate waste. It is the sneak-thief destroyer and whoring accomplice of corroding time, the cruel and malign marauder of humanity's sweet hopes. The one proof that the world is not yet civilized is that we continue to indulge in it. One cannot say too much against war. Jesus is right, all the great religious teachers like Gandhi are right, in declaring it a method of madness and no way out at all for man and his troubles. Rather it only adds to these troubles, intensifies and magnifies them. These teachers are right when they say that the one way to get rid of war with its killings, burnings, and mutilations is to renounce force forever as a practice among men, have nothing to do with violence—be a conscientious objector like you, if you will. It is hard for a thoughtful kindly man to stomach war with its rot and stench and vomit of blood, and the more so if he happens to have an extra touch of the artist's urge and sensitivity as you have. Twenty-five years ago when I enlisted in the first world war I believed it true and I believe it now.

But when a nation or group of nations embark seriously on the business of war, all decorations, all sensitivities, beauties, aesthetic cravings, functions and soarings of the creative spirit must immediately stand before the court of Practical Use and be tried. And without exception they, in times past as well as now, are found guilty of vagrancy. Sometimes the sentence is light, sometimes severe, depending on the tempo of the crisis and the temper of the judge. But always there is some sort of sentence, some penalty to be meted out.

For war deals with the prime, basic animal fact of survival one over against the other, no matter what ideals or shibboleths of glory have been shouted or prayed into it before it got down to a matter of "their life or ours," "his or mine." Now the artist does not deal with these purely physical and combative facts as such. Like the true religionist, his aspirations, his visions and accomplishments live in another realm. But it happens that he also is a physical being, a citizen, man or woman, a member of the battling group on one side or the other and by the very nature of time and circumstance involved in the happenings around him. Whether he will it or not, he must somehow partake of the fight, carrying on his art the while, if need be in little wishes and wordless hopes, in little side-of-the-road deeds and devotions as best he can. While the fight thunders, the demands on him are not and cannot be as an artist but as a physical being and member of the social fighting group. Nor can he ignore these demands if he is to participate fully in the life that follows—when the fight is over and the creative and rebuilding ways of peace are active again.

In the aloofness of your logic no doubt you are right in your conscientious-objector attitude. But emotionally, spiritually, and as a citizen of a practical world you are wrong. And if you had the power, which you haven't, of withdrawing from among your fellows, your comrades of the everyday time, and standing separate and alone above the swelter and the turmoil and the ultimate risk—the risk, don't forget that and what that means psychologically and ethically to a man—you would likely "perish" as an artist later on from this same withdrawal and ego solitude.

It is a soul-and-body problem after all, isn't it? And the body takes its physical precedence here, has to. So I don't see any real honest-to-goodness decision to be made on your part except one that will propel you along with your

fellows into your proper share not of the guilt but of the
risk of war. God knows the risk of a tragic and wasteful
sort is here when you have to give over your inspired
writing for carrying a gun to kill an enemy who might
well be your friend in more blessed and brighter days.
But as a man it seems you must do that very thing—if for
no other reason than to help guarantee the welfare and
growth of your art itself in the future. Baffling and queer
that it should be so.

Now believe me I'm not preaching such foolishness
here as that a man should serve the devil for a while in
order to serve God better later on. Or that one should beat
his wife on Monday so that he might love her more and
with a difference on Tuesday, as Tennyson seems to have
it in the little song that says. . . .

> As through the land at eve we went,
> And plucked the ripened ears,
> We fell out my wife and I,
> O we fell out I know not why
> And kissed again with tears.
> And blessings on the falling out
> That all the more endears.

No, it's all deeper than that, tragically and not senti-
mentally or comically or melodramatically deeper. It's a
question of moral freedom of the individual soul, isn't it?
Now you claim to be living under a (democratic) dispensation of freedom of choice for conscience sake and thus
you can make the decision to become a conscientious objector and pay the price demanded of you. But there is
already spiritually and practically a predestination for
you in the "common pull."

As a normal being, and the true artist is that or nothing,

one cannot be happy and free in irresponsibility when others all around him are loaded with responsibility. The demand that men share alike as comrades in the group experience, in the common risk, is too strong. Thomas Hardy says something about how "If a way to the better there be, it exacts a full look at the worst," which might be amended for our purpose to read "If a way to the better there be, it exacts a full *share* of the worst."

I know that all kinds of our folk sayings, proverbs, and daily snitches of wisdom's images could be invoked to blast this argument, if it is an argument—such as, "Can you save a burning building by adding to the flames?", "Can you become innocent by first becoming guilty?", "Can you purge the crime by being a criminal?", etc., etc., on around to the reference above of the serving of God and beating one's wife. But these are not real and responsible rebuttals.

For logically prior to all of them and continuing when they are ended, are the facts, namely, that we are now involved in a terrific war. There is no turning back. We cannot find God, peace, and creative work again except through the bloody meadow forward and over the stile of trampled flowers, on by the mourner's bench, the wailing wall, and across the corpse-glutted ditch to the green upland waiting. The "enemy" is there opposite, against us. It is now either he or we. Such is the tragedy and the waste of the thing, and such is its all-compelling, its mystic, and awful necessity.

We must fight on to victory and the new day, and we need you, John, to fight with us. For in the summation later that seems the only way you and I can guarantee the return of our lives into the full flower and fruitage for

which they were meant. Even then the guarantee may fail,
yet I for one know nothing else to do.

But O the bleeding drops of red, the dark stain on the
ground!

Yes, with Aeschylus let us weep.

Dialogue At Evening

CRITIC: (*As they stroll.*) This play must have been an undertaking. (*He gestures towards an outdoor theatre near by.*)

AUTHOR: It was.

"What with that huge stockade around the fort, and the blockhouse, the chapel, the cabins, the amphitheatre, the stage, the dressing rooms and all."

"And the water system, hot and cold."

"That, too. It must have been a lot of work."

"It was, and a lot of folks did it."

"How many people would you say have been involved in the project?"

"Counting the workers, the actors, the technicians, and the citizens of the island, I should say about a thousand. Maybe more from first to last."

"Remarkable. It's a real community endeavor, isn't it?"

"Yes."

"But a little puzzling to find a venture like this down in a lonely country and so far from civilization."

"I don't know about that."

"About what?"

"About being so far from civilization."

"Hm-mn. Well, I mean so far from any big city. Norfolk is the nearest large town, isn't it?"

"Yes, about ninety miles away."

"That's what I thought. Where do your audiences come from?"

"They come from everywhere, like you and me."

"Yes, but I have a sort of professional reason for coming. I am a critic."

"The people come unprofessionally and because they want to see the show."

"Oh, yes. Of course. Do you plan to run it year after year?"

"Yes, that is the intent of those in charge. We will continue it as long as the public will support it. I hope it will be going fifty years from now."

"I hope your hopes will be realized, but—" (*Staring off across the sound at the solitary Wright Memorial and the sand dunes in the distance.*) "It's a lonely country all right. Look at that water there in the sound—motionless, smooth as glass. Life stands still."

"But sometimes it cuts up."

"What?"

"The sound."

"You wouldn't think it. How do your New York actors like it here?"

"Most of them want to come back each year."

"And how do they get along with the natives?"

"After a few weeks you can't tell them from the islanders."

"What do the people do for a living here?"

"They farm a little, hunt, fish, do coast guard work, and in the summer put on the play and take care of the people who come to see it."

"And now about the play itself. How did *The Lost Colony* come to be produced in the first place?"

"I hardly know. I suppose it was because the people on Roanoke Island wanted it and worked for it. For a long while they had held some sort of local celebration off and on each August 18th in honor of Virginia Dare's birthday."

"Virginia Dare?"

"In the school books it tells how she was the first child born of English parents in the New World."

"I remember now. It has been so long ago."

"Yes, we all forget. That's why plays are written, so we won't, don't you think?"

"Perhaps. And then?"

"Well, the island people took the initiative in the matter. Led by our local Mr. D. B. Fearing and aided by Mr. W. O. Saunders, an editor from Elizabeth City (that's a town up in the mainland) they all set about preparing plans for a 350th anniversary celebration to memorialize Sir Walter Raleigh's lost colony and Virginia Dare. One of the plans was to hold a nationwide beauty contest to select the girl who should play Virginia Dare. At that time they didn't know, nor did I, that when the play came to be written she would be a baby and remain so. In all our minds was the legend that she grew up to be a beautiful maiden, fell in love with the Indian chief Manteo's son, married him, and became the mother of a brave race that somehow evaporated into thin air. As Mr. Fearing, Mr. Saunders, and others went on with their work, I who had always been interested in the romantic and tragic story of these early colonists joined with them. But our combined efforts produced little more than pledges of money and coöperation, and with the deepening of the depression they amounted to little. Then came the W. P. A. and saved us. Mr. Fearing and his helpers got a project approved to build the theatre, and I set about writing the play. With the aid of Congressman Lindsay Warren, 25,000 memorial fifty-cent coins were minted by the United States which were sold to collectors for a dollar and a half each. Through this means some funds were raised to pay the necessary proportion of materials for the project. And so we were started. But only started, for as the size of the production grew the need for more money increased. The night we opened we were deeply in debt. At least Mr. Fearing and certain local business men were."

"And the production paid out?"

"Yes."

"You were lucky."

"We all were. If it hadn't been for the W. P. A. and the Federal Theatre—"

"Well, we can leave that out. You know how my paper feels about the New Deal. And now what do you consider to be the main factors in the success of the play?"

"The main reason was that our business manager and key man, Mr. D. B. Fearing, was a confirmed and energetic optimist. No sight of bad luck or fear of failure could stop him. Also another reason was that the local people were interested both as helpers and as active participants in the show. Then we had a fine and understanding director in Mr. Samuel Selden, a devoted builder in Mr. Albert Q. Bell, and a gifted newspaper man in Mr. Ben Dixon MacNeill who throughout the first summer kept writing vivid and human interest stories about the production. And finally the music, color, and movement of the play itself attracted the public. And those who came kept passing the word along to others. These were the main reasons, I suppose—not forgetting the technicians and actors, of course."

"I notice in the program here you call *The Lost Colony* a symphonic drama. Is it because you have music in it?"

"No, not primarily. I have used the phrase to describe one or two other plays I've written. It's not a perfect-fitting term but the best I can find, better than music or musical drama. In the original sense it means "sounding together." That is, all the elements of the theatre working together— music, song, dance, pantomime, etc."

"It's something new, isn't it?"

"No, it's pretty much as old as drama itself. The Greeks and the people of medieval and Elizabethan England produced outdoor plays like this. And years ago Percy Mackaye wrote and produced masques and pageants somewhat like it."

"Do you call it a pageant or a play?"

"A play. For it tells a story, and the characters are individuals, not types, as is usually the case in masques and pageants."

"Do you think the idea will spread and other localities will produce such plays?"

"I hope so. It seems to me there is a great chance for this kind of drama in America. This is a vast country full of legends and rich in story and song—all waiting to be used. And with the convenience of the automobile there is no reason why audiences cannot be drawn to any place if there's a colorful and interesting show to be seen. And there's something about a production outdoors that seems to fit the temper of the American people—maybe all people for that matter. Within the next few years I hope to see hundreds of summer dramatic festivals and productions scattered over the land from coast to coast. That would be one more way of making our people's lives vivid and more worth while. Then maybe we would begin to have a real people's theatre."

"I've heard a great deal of talk in my time about a people's theatre. What do you mean by it?"

"I mean a theatre in which plays are written, acted, and produced for and by the people—for their enjoyment and enrichment and not for any special monetary profit. Then when the country becomes theatre-minded, the level of taste and appreciation will gradually rise higher and higher. And some day the mountain peaks of drama— men like Aeschylus, Lope de Vega, and Shakespeare— will rise on the solid base beneath. As long as the American drama stays bottled up in the narrow neck and cul-de-sac of Broadway we can expect nothing better than what we have. I don't mean bottled up exactly, for already groups and sections of the country are turning their backs on the professional theatre and beginning to write and produce their own plays and the plays of others in a style equal to the best. For instance, the finest production of *The Cherry Orchard* I ever saw was at the University of Iowa some years ago."

"But surely you don't think the amateur theatre can measure up to the high standards of Broadway generally?"

"I don't know how high the standards of Broadway are generally, but the amateur theatre not only can measure up to them, but will, and more and more so as time goes on. The decentralization of the theatre has already set in."

"I don't share your enthusiasm there. Nothing bores me so much as an amateur play. Frankly that's why I'm not so sure I'm going to like *The Lost Colony*. From the list here it seems there are too many amateurs in it."

"They're not theatre people. Most of them have other jobs to do and they act for the pleasure in it. I think they're wise. When you consider the thousands of young people wearing out their fathers' shoe leather tramping the fruitless pavement of Broadway, and think of the fine things they might be doing back in their home neighborhood or town—"

"Frankly I think you are unfair to Broadway. You've never looked at it justly nor given it a real try. You ought to, you know, for your own sake as a writer."

"Oh, I hope to continue writing plays for Broadway now and then."

"But that's not the way to do it. You must throw yourself whole-heartedly into it."

"I've thought a lot about that, too."

"And what sort of answer did you arrive at?"

"This." (*With a gesture.*)

"Oh, well—" (*Looking at his watch.*) "It must be about time for the show to start."

"It is." (*He stares off at the wide western sky.*)

"Are you planning any other productions like this?" (*They turn.*)

"One I've thought about a great deal is to be in western North Carolina—that is, if we can find some business men up there willing to take the financial risk. I want to see the most beautiful outdoor theatre in the world built there on a mountain top close to the stars. And with the music, song, ballad, and dance of the people as material to work from, a beautiful and inspiring play can be done. Already I imagine great crowds of people coming from the south and from the north, moving along the skyline drive of the eastern world, all coming to see it."

"Aren't you a bit optimistic in your seeing?"

"It's nothing but a dream, I know. But some day—"

"Well, good luck. (*As a great diapason of sound suddenly breaks across the twilight.*) There, I hear the organ. Sounds rather nice."

"It sounds wonderful to me."

(*They go up towards the theatre.*)

Children by the Waterside

O children by the waterside,
Lift up your harps and sing!

1

MEN DREAMED A DREAM—AND NOT SO LONG AGO—
and out of that dreaming contrived them marvels never
seen on land or sea. So they did. They put their fierce im-
print on nature's handiwork and fashioned forth the
miracle we call machines. And they walked about wrapped
in the wonder of their creating, delighting in their work
like God himself and finding it good. The perfect wheel
was made, the lank sleeveless piston arm, and the squat
engine to energize and move them both. The wing was
added to the wheel, the lightning bolted in, and the tur-
bines set to spin their thread of light over the prairies, over
the mountains and into whatever lonely homes.

And everywhere along the earth and in the earth these
machines, these creatures of man's dreaming, were put to

work to do his will and labor in his stead. And the children of sweat and lightless gaze, the broken and despairing ones, all that interminable and ancient line of the world's slaves who lived to work and worked to die glimpsed the ending of their slavery. And a shout of joy broke across the gloom, growing into a *te deum*, swelling into an anthem of jubilation. And there out to heaven's gates went the song of man freed at last and master of himself. And far to the east and to the west, to the north and to the south, the dawn of a new day broke over the beauteous and smiling world.

2

But in the evening when the dreamer and the tired ones slept the adversary came with his cohorts of greed and plunder and gained possession of the machines and turned them against their fellows once again. And that which was made for good became the instrument of pain and death. Freedom's cry became again the slave's lament. Too short the tale to tell, too long to be listened to.

And so the days have passed, the years have come and gone, and the voice of the taskmaster and the groan of the oppressed continue on the earth. And ever the adversary and his machines grow mightier, ever more fitted for the ways of sin and death.

Where is the life they could provide? Where the abundant life that they would build?

3

Over the horizon that cuts to the east and there beyond the horizon that cuts to the west the attentive and mournful listener can hear the tramp of martial feet, the clamor of wrath and woe and the confusion of men undone. And grieving in the small hours, he may likewise look over the horizon to the north and beyond the horizon to the south, and beating upon his ears will come the same distressful sounds of angry steel upon steel and the cries of unhappy folk fighting to death for privilege and rights denied. Despair and desolation, horror and apocalypse, even the four horsemen known of old, are riding hard once more over the mute and piteous world. And now in these latter days it would seem that some other listener—He whom the pulpit preachers praise—might well turn His face away and leave the race of men to destroy themselves and give the earth over to kindly animals and flowers and trees and birds again.

For we are madmen now, madder than before.

4

Long, long ago the dreamers came into this land—men of all creeds and nations—rich men, poor men, beggarmen, thieves;—wanderers, tipsters, the weak of will, the hard of fist;—the soft men, the iron men, the servant and the slave—all seeking a newer life, a better day, a wider scope for their endeavor and their dream. Flight from persecution, hunger for adventure, thirst for gold, desire for power, fear of power—myriad the causes that brought them here.

And what did they find here?—a vast wilderness stretching tree above tree, hill above hill, river beyond river, plain across plain ever westward towards the setting sun. This was their challenge, this their destiny—man in the wilderness, man against the wilderness. There it stood and there he stood—sizing each other up, measuring their manhood, feeling their muscle, bragging and daring and boasting of victory.

And the struggle was on. Chop-chop went the axes. Chop-chop—clearing and building. The crashing and booming and bounding of mighty falling trees was heard, of the strong-hearted giant trees. And the days passed—chop-chop—the years passed, the generations came and went. And each succeeding was a little stronger, a little surer, a little more certain—a little freer as they chopped and cleared and fashioned and shaped. You must tame me or perish, sang the wilderness, tame me or die.

And ever the ears listened and the muscles sprang!

And the headman rose up and took his place—and led the slow march, the slow creeping migration upward from the sea, slowly upward from the sea. Chop-chop-chop. And behind them the fields appeared, the hamlets grew. And dancing and laughter and singing were heard—at the birthing, at the reaping, in the halls of counsel and by the fireside. And the race grew strong as the wilderness was strong, grew free as the wilderness was wide.

But this was not enough. Creation was at work. And the towns appeared, cities grew, shipping and trading and a world of traffic poured back and forth, and the need for government came to be. And on a day the headmen, now grown old, met and spoke forth their speech, said their say of the wilderness and the wisdom they had seen. And the poets wrote it down, and the singers sang it across the land. Morning, noon, and night they sang, and ever the refrain

was heard—a nation of liberty and free men and justice
unto all.

5

O children by the waterside,
Lift up your harps and sing!

━━━

The Dying American Theatre

1

THERE HAS BEEN A LOT OF WRITING AND TALK OF
recent years about the decline of the American theatre.
And any look at the present condition of Broadway would
seem to show that much of this writing and talk is justified.
Scores of our best playwrights, musicians, actors, directors, producers, artists, technicians, and designers, grown
discouraged over repeated failures of their plays around
Times Square, already have long ago departed the scene
for other parts and jobs well-known. And the thinning
ranks of those left behind to carry on the struggle are pretty
much downhearted over the spectacle of a great people's
art perishing before their eyes. And they too as occasion
comes continue to leave one by one to join their brothers
and sisters in other business enterprises or in Hollywood
or some radio studio where they can hope to draw a steady
and honest workman's wage from a safe and going concern.

Pessimism pretty general and heavy hangs over the

109

once great white way. You can read it so in any fat metropolitan daily on any bright Sabbath morning. The theatre is not only declining, some say, but is dying and has been for a long time. Others openly declare that it is not dying but dead. The facts speak for themselves. And if you are inclined to argue the point, as I am, they will disgorge for your and the public's benefit a splurge of depreciative statistics which they in their discouragement have gathered up. And the few who remain unconvinced and optimistic still, alas, are only a few, and growing fewer. So it seems.

Now what are some of these facts? Is the American theatre really dying? Is this great art which some of us think is the noblest and most complete of all the arts in its active and enriching imaginative power, in its full and vitalizing use of all the other arts inside its fold—is it on its last legs? Do the signs all say so? And had the few faithful workers in it just as well give over their wishes and dreams for an inspiring dramatic interpretation of their country and its meaning, of their people and their age, and count them off as lost along with the multitudinous dramatic "movements" and groups and individual endeavors that have risen, flourished for a moment, and died?

Yes, we might as well do that very thing, said a well-known dramatic writer and historian to me recently. He was on his way to Florida for a rest and stopped off in our little Southern village for a few days to take things easy and see the breaking spring of Carolina. For a quarter of a century and more this man has been writing books and articles about the American theatre. Through all its ups and downs he has followed it, loved it—criticizing, interpreting, appraising, prophesying and holding out hopes for it, which hopes, he said to me on this occasion, he has seen die one by one. Now he declares he is worn out with it all, disillusioned and hopeless about it. Around the fire one evening in my farmhouse and over a highball he let fly his frank feelings on the subject. And bitter as it was I had to agree with much of what he said. While the March night wind moaned and nibbled around the house he went on talking about it all.

2

Yes, he said, the great figures of high dramatic enterprise are all dead or fled and only the little traders in the temple are left alive. Indeed the temple itself throughout the width and breadth of this land has been torn down and a gaudy emporium repeated in replica a thousand times erected in its stead. So let us turn away from futile repining and go get our jobs in the entertainment industries of the movie and radio. For these are what the people want and pay to see and hear. The overwhelming facts assert it. You go get the job, I mean, I am too old.

For while the art of the theatre stands bankrupt, the movies and radio through thick and thin continue to thrive, and they have been thriving for lo these many years. There is no sign that they are weakening and if they did weaken there is no proof that such weakening would help the theatre the least bit. Rather the contrary perhaps, he said. The bent of the times is different now and the theatre fails to fit in. The movies and radio do, and television will. Speed and machinery and mass-made entertainment are the go. The theatre is too slow, too unwieldy and expensive for value received. Its confines are now too narrow for high-powered American ambition. The bold souls have had to desert Broadway for a wider and more profitable field for their endeavors. Such names as Jed Harris, Arthur Hopkins, Lee Shubert, Hermann Shumlin, Guthrie McClintic, Theresa Helburn, Brock Pemberton, Cheryl Crawford, to pick at random, can't compare in influence and importance today with a Sarnoff, Warner, Goldwyn, Wanger, Selznick, Mayer, Zanuck, or even Schenck. These last are the entertainment producing names that count with the American public.

And in front of all and brighter by far than any of these are the scores of radio and movie stars. It's true that in the theatre we still have the fine personalities of Helen Hayes, Katharine Cornell, Alfred Lunt, Lynn Fontanne, Judith Anderson, Jane Cowl, Ruth Gordon, and one or two others. But they pretty well exhaust the crop. They are the lone survivors in a beleaguered and falling citadel, whereas there are hundreds of screen and radio actors and actresses whose names are on the lips of millions of Americans, of Americans who have never heard the names of any of those actors mentioned above except by way of an occasional movie or over the radio. In any hamlet or town the men, women, and children, whether Rotarian, D. A. R., or scout, carry daily in their minds the character, dress, and likeness of Gary Cooper, Joan Crawford, Mickey Rooney, Betty Grable, Errol Flynn, Clark Gable, Rita Hayworth, Ginger Rogers, Bob Hope, James Cagney, and ninety-nine or a thousand others. These are the manikins and minikins who fashion and shape much of the thinking and ideals of our citizenry. These they copy by. Yes, I agree in passing, that the hamlets and towns and crossroads also are acquainted with Donald Duck, Pluto, and Mickey Mouse, though they are forgetting Charlie Chaplin. Nothing can be so bad that there isn't some good in it.

But the fact remains, the historian continued, that while we poor fellows of the theatre gather emptily together, eat our sandwich, and talk our desperate talk about the art we love, the two great mediums of the movies and the radio, and television soon to be, continue to swell full-panoplied, all-tooled and powerful, close by the clicking money-till in front of where the female wonder is. And if it's not the lady wonder then it is some other commodity or gadget to be sold in tuneful ballyhoo—vegetable compounds, alkalis, or chewing gum. In Mr. Einstein's phrase, the movie kings and radio moguls have a world line of their own and follow it. They're on the beam, they know the answers, their jive is hot, they're in the groove. Listen, friend, I'm telling you the facts.

And so he went on telling me. Yes, these magnates have absorbed the theatre business. The gullible public eats from their hand. And why not? For they scratch the public where it itches. Look out through the hotel window in any town and watch the populace crowd by, all in a line to see, say, Barbara Stanwyck in her Ball of Fire, or Dorothy Lamour or Hedy Lamarr crooning to a cart-wheel love-sick moon, or some athletic young American caliph lying turbaned and confined in a harem's expectant bed. That's the way it is, I say. And farther up the street there you may see the tail end of another line a block long where the boys and girls, the young and old, are pushing in to see the bombers crashing and blazing and great ships breaking in two, to hear the rattle of machine guns, the explosions of bombs, and squealing shells in predestined studio defeat

of the Nazis and treacherous Japanese by artless democratic brawn.

Yes, they've got what it takes to stake off the world,
interpret its easy whimsies and describe it. We haven't.
These tycoons of the movies and radio like Ephraim in the
song have caught the coon and gone on, and we don't even
smell what's cooking. Yes, I know the language too. We
can't compete against them. Our homestead, birthright,
and pottage pot now belong to them. We should have seen
it coming long ago and sold for the highest possible price.
But we didn't, and now we're left holding the empty bag.
Then why sit any longer dreaming of our pitiful and cir-
cumscribed little plays and all the swarm of attendant
theatrical difficulties of rents, royalties, unions, equity,
carpentry, haulage, and the Lord knows what, which pre-
cludes the risk of a production one time in a hundred.
Give the author back his script, close up, and let's be gone
from here. There is no doubt about it. Broadway and the
American theatre are as good as dead.

And if you are still unconvinced by these arguments
and still believe that the theatre remains a powerful force
in American life, as you say, I will grow more specific and
frank in the proof of my contention, he said.

Take the case of the American playwrights. Where are
they? I ask you. What has happened to them? What has
happened to you, lost down here in the woods? For without good playwrights you can have no sort of theatre. They
are the first and foremost element that goes into its making.
Call the roll and like the others they don't answer. Let us
be frank now and away with hurt feelings and hypocrisy.
A spade is a spade, and a funeral a funeral. Most of them
have left Broadway, gone on a journey, turned to writing

for these same movies and radio commodities, taken up the novel, or become poets if they are writing still. True they come back, but only occasionally, and with ever increasing delay between trips, with a play for Broadway. And nearly every time the play they bring is weaker than the one they offered before. Their energies and inspiration have been scattered. Others have quit the game altogether for real estate, brokerage business, life insurance, law, teaching, editing, or what not. And the recent call of patriotism doesn't change the truth of my argument. No, the American playwrights have failed us, and they were the first to fail when they should have been the last, if failure was to be.

Where are all the bright portents of writing genius we thought we saw in the twenties and thirties? Have they not proved to be flashes in the pan or tokens of a false dawn only? Where are the dozen or more young Eugene O'Neills prophesied and proclaimed of recent years in the public press? They turned out to be easily discouraged, young men of one play promise, or at most two and the second usually less vital than the first. With one shot they had fired their wad. Yes, I know it happens with our novelists and poets too, but not to the same consistent and discouraging degree. And where is O'Neill himself? Real and vital as were the plays he gave us, we all still expected something finer to come, something more authoritative and charged more fully with life's wisdom.

Go typically down the line if you will, and the story sounds the same, the same early promise and subsequent lack of fulfilment. Consider Maxwell Anderson. He may seem to be an exception to the rule, for he has kept on writing steadfastly for the stage. But is he? Some eighteen years ago along with Laurence Stallings he burst in on Broadway with the powerful and dynamic *What Price Glory*. Here was a great new talent. Here were new and exciting American characters created on the stage—Sergeant Quirt and Captain Flagg. A gallery of others were to come. But they haven't come. Since that time Anderson hasn't created a single character that has made any comparable impression on American taste and interest. His semi- and pseudo-poetic excursions into English and American history have in the main only dressed up well-known names without recreating or deepening of the nature or our understanding of the characters behind those names. They entertained us slightly for a while and then passed on over the river to lie with the characters of Stephen Phillips and Clyde Fitch forgotten and asleep. You have only to compare his current *Eve of St. Mark*, small, quiet, and abrupt as it is, with its striding first world war predecessor to make the measurement of what we mean. There's not a single character in *The Eve of St. Mark* that one remembers for a day.

And Phillip Barry? Years ago he gave us his rather original and eager *Hotel Universe*. That, too, promised much to come. But the promise still waits. He is now reduced to one string only, thin and easy, and one actress only. And Marc Connelly, who by way of Roark Bradford created one of the finest of modern folk-morality plays in *The Green Pastures*? He has never come near that mark since. Sidney Howard long ago wrote a splendid neo-Ibsen play in *The Silver Cord*. That too remained the tops above all his subsequent efforts. In George Kelly's *Show-Off*, now nearly twenty years old, we had one of the best American comedies ever written. High praise and a great expectancy were cloaked around him. Certainly on my part there were. Then after a few other weakening attempts he quit discouraged and wrote farewell—still a very young man in the prime of what ought to have been his powers—to Broadway and his theatre dreams. John Howard Lawson sired out of German Expressionism a promising play, *Roger Bloomer,* and his *Processional* suggested better things to come. But these better things haven't shown up. Clifford Odets, whom Heywood Broun in a misguided but understandable loyalty heralded as greater than O'Neill, wrote his *Awake and Sing* in the full flush of his youth and self-certain strength. Still after half a dozen other long plays his first remains his best by far.

Elmer Rice, one of the most faithful and tough-fibred adherents of the theatre, long ago gave us his fine, German, too, expressionist play, *The Adding Machine,* and some years later his truly American and metropolitan people's drama in *Street Scene.* Many others have come from him since then, including the lately revived *Counselor-at-Law,* but there seems to have been a steady decline in his work now for several years. William Saroyan is a late-comer, and in his first Broadway success, *My Heart's in the Highlands,* we had the same old ballyhoo and build-up of the critics. Here again was the familiar portent of the white hope, the promise of the American theatre. He followed this play with a flurry of others, written as he apparently pleases to say like Lope de Vega, each between a breakfast and a noon, or in a single night. We may believe his statement, for his plays are beginning to look like it. With a growing carelessness as to character and story form, as his self-confidence increases, he is apparently inviting his own disaster and failure from within.

In Robert Sherwood, Broadway has had one of its finest talents. The critics generally agree that he stands next to O'Neill in his sincerity, strength of plot, and character creation. I at least think he does. Though certainly lacking the literary and poetical gift of O'Neill, he has nevertheless a fine sense of dialogue and construction and a sensitive eye and feel for stage emphasis and business. His *Reunion in Vienna,* written some twelve years ago, remains one of the high accomplishments in the American theatre. Original, wise, sophisticated, and thorough in its exploration of character, idea, and situation, it brought to our drama the master European touch. What a far cry from it back to the empty and imitative work of James A. Herne, a Bronson Howard, a Thomas, Gillette, or even Edward Sheldon. At last with O'Neill and Sherwood the American theatre was growing up, it seemed, and now we were on our way to greater things. But Sherwood too has run pretty much to the form of failure. Like the others he has become static or declined in his powers. His *Abe Lincoln in Illinois,* though tremendously popular and appealing, showed no first-rate creative work either in character or story. It was a rather easy job of dramatizing and shaping historical material already well formed and available from life itself. The actual character of Lincoln in action as we already surmised and loved him was what interested the public and not what the playwright creatively gave to that character. In fact there was little or no creation in the play. In his topical and impassioned propaganda piece, *There Shall Be No Night,* Sherwood recently and for a while revived the hopeful spark in his work. Perhaps there is a chance yet that he will come through after his service in the war with a fulfillment of his earlier promise. Again the word "promise."

These are some of our best playwrights, though not all, and you see what has happened with them, I say, the historian went on. And the same discouraging sizing-up will apply to others—Atlas, Behrman, Boothe, Conkle, Davis, Hart, Hellman, Heyward, Hughes, Kaufman, Kingsley, Lindsay, Raphaelson, Riggs, Stallings, Turney, Vollmer, and Wexley. None of them has shown the real thing in growth and deepening development. Too, most of them are occasional playwrights, and those that are steady and prolific don't do much more than repeat themselves. I ask you, do they? John Steinbeck and Thornton Wilder who have more lately come upon the scene are primarily novelists. Steinbeck's two plays, *Of Mice and Men* and *The Moon is Down*, were written out of his two novels of the same names. They show no particular interest in the stage on the part of the author nor any great talent for it. Thornton Wilder has written two astonishingly experimental plays with great theatrical authority and skill, *Our Town* and *The Skin of Our Teeth*. What else is to come from him I don't know, but it seems significant again to notice that the second play is incomparably poorer in vitality and humanity than the first. We would hazard a guess that his third and fourth will be poorer still, and he will turn again to his novels. So it goes.

Yes, the case of the American playwrights offers no cause at all for optimism about the future, my friend reiterated dolefully. Indeed—yes, we are thankful for what we have had, but I must insist that the playwrights have given us neither the quality nor quantity of plays we had a right to expect, what their early work promised us. They have been handicapped, hindered and confined for some reason or other and have not grown to the full stature of creative artists as they should. Are the radio and movies entirely to blame? Perhaps so, perhaps not. But whatever the reason, we know they have failed our hopes for them which once were so high.

And as they have failed, so of necessity all the other theatre arts and artists have failed and been denied their proper chance. There is no need here to cover the list of these from the Barrymores to Blanche Yurka among the actors, from Boris Aronson to Cleon Throckmorton among the designers, from George Abbott to Dwight Deere Wiman among the producers, or from Anthony Brown to Orson Welles among the directors. Their story is the same. They have had to depend on the playwrights for material to work with, and the playwrights have not come through. So these artists have been frustrated and deprived, and their hopes and plans and purposes gone glimmering on paper or died image-faded and wordless in their heads. Think of the vast projects that Norman Bel Geddes has dreamed and schemed after. Consider the visions and plannings of Joseph Urban. Where are the actual accomplishments in the imaginative drama that Robert Edmond Jones has spent most of his life trying to see realized? Nowhere. None of these gifted men has been sustained and buoyed up by a playwright with a talent and integrity equal or comparable to their need. They still wait and will continue to wait the genius they had a right to look for. By this time they must know he will never come, not in their lifetime. No wonder they too are having to turn to engineering, architecture, and furniture designing, piddling some and making notes and writing little theatre essays in their dismay and emptiness of days, and all to ease themselves.

And if you're not convinced by this time that the American theatre is dying or dead, let me but add a few final and more specific facts, he said. There are today in New York City some seven thousand actors, or were until Uncle Sam began to take care of some of them, all waiting around, wearing out their skirts and britches in some manager's office, or pitifully walking their shoe leather off on the sidewalks looking for jobs that never come. Some seven thousand, mind you, when in any one season there are never more than a scant few hundred jobs available, and only for a few weeks at that, so small has the demand become, and daily becoming smaller. They live wretchedly from hand to mouth, borrowing money from this friend or that, picking up this crumb of hope here and there as best they can. And they're fine American citizens, young and old, with a lot of talent too. There simply is no place for them, and like the other followers of Broadway they haven't learned it yet.

And the same thing applies to the young and unknown aspiring playwrights. Thousands of plays are written year after year—seventy-five thousand in the United States last year according to the figures I have gathered—and not one in five thousand ever gets a Broadway hearing. Maybe they shouldn't, of course. Most of them aren't worth the paper they're written on anyway. But why can't the best of them be heard? Because there is no place to produce them in. And if there were, the difficulties of production, as I said, have become so great that you can find a manager only now and then who will take the risk. He is snooping, forever snooping for a sure-fire success. He cannot afford to experiment, as he puts it. Between the real-estate and union demands the poor shivering author is stymied, and the play he poured his life's blood into is left to be eaten up by termites or whatever it is that feeds on manuscripts.

Twenty-five years ago, my friend gloomily went on, there were some five thousand professional theatres and opera buildings thickly dotting the map of the United States. Hardly a town of ten thousand or more but had its local playhouse. In them the best Broadway professional and stock companies offered the latest and finest in the world's theatrical art. Current European as well as American plays were given—oh, yes, along with the tripe too. And there were musicals and operas. Here Shakespeare, Molière, Sheridan, Ibsen, Scribe, Maeterlinck, Rostand, and even Shaw were shown. In New York City alone there were, I estimate, three hundred such theatre buildings. Boston, Chicago, Philadelphia, Washington, Baltimore, San Francisco, and other cities had their dozens. Where are they today? Gone, torn down. In the whole country there are less than a hundred left, and half of them remain in New York. Yes, the theatre no longer has a home. So homeless it must die.

Well, that's the way the story runs, my friend, the discouraged scholar and historian concluded, and I see nothing that can be done about it except to say goodbye and gone to it all and turn our minds to other things. How is the winter climate here in Carolina? I am hunting a place to retire to. I want to build myself a modest home where it's warm, settle down, raise flowers and chickens

perhaps and write my big book summing it up and putting
a period to it so far as I am concerned. How is it?

3

Although I tried to argue against the logic of fact which
my friend deluged me with, he would have none of it.
Nothing I said made any impression on him. His mind
was closed. And when finally I pointed vehemently to the
work of the amateur theatre in America, or people's
theatre as I like to call it, he threw up his hands in anathema, smote the air and said we'd call it a night. And we did.

Now there's no doubt about it, the facts he unrolled for
me were convincing and discouraging enough, all right.
And if there hadn't been another side to it all, I too would
have had to give in before him. But there is another side,
and I discovered it during my travels of the last few years
around the country, away from Broadway. The trouble
with this theatre pessimist as with all the others is that
though their facts are logical enough their premise is all
wrong. That is what I discovered. They are like Hitler in
his *Mein Kampf*. That is a powerful book and devastating
in its logic once you accept the declaration of government
and citizenship underlying it. But there the trouble is. Its
so-called axioms and basic truths are completely contrary
to any sound philosophy of history and the idealistic nature of striving man. The wider view, the universal human
need, is narrowed down to fit what the Nazis call a German
and racial truth. So they make the old mistake of missing
the woods and cracking their heads against the trees. Likewise my friend and his fellows much the same. Their mistake lies in their continuing to identify the American

theatre with Broadway, when such identification is no longer possible. Twenty-five years ago it might have been true, it was true. But it certainly is so no longer.

The American theatre today is not on Broadway but in the thousands upon thousands of amateur and non-professional groups in the hamlets and towns, in the granges, the high schools, the colleges, universities, trade union halls, army posts, and in the civic centers everywhere. It is the theatre of the whole vast United States. And we ought to be thankful that this is so, be thankful that the narrow confines, the bottleneck of Times Square no more is sufficient for the clamor and urge to self-expression among our people. Where there were once five thousand theatre stages in the country and all an extension of Broadway and its syndicalists, now there are twenty-five, thirty, even fifty thousand, built and created by the people themselves for their own needs, their feelings, purposes and vision. And here night after night they act and see acted and set forth in all intensity and sincerity dramas and stories of their own choosing and often of their own writing. Though many of these plays and their productions may be crude and uncomfortably naïve, they are still their own and have a close and enriching meaning to them. And always the quality is improving. The finest Chekhov production I ever saw, and I have seen many, was given by E. C. Mabie's group at the University of Iowa some summers ago. The dramatic work of Gilmor Brown at the Pasadena Playhouse, of Frederic McConnell at The Cleveland Playhouse, of Frederick H. Koch and Samuel Selden at the University of North Carolina, of Alexander Drummond at Cornell University, of Glenn Hughes in his two theatres at Seattle, of Arthur Cloetingh at Pennsylvania State College, of Gordon Giffin and Dorothy Heyward at The Dock Street Theatre in Charleston, South Carolina, of Jasper Deeter at the Hedgerow Theatre, and of many, many others is more often than not equal to the highest standard of professional excellence. And even if it were not what final difference would it make, since it all is in the process of development, a sure development and a sure finding of its way? Here is a vast and growing theatre, rugged and dynamic in its nature, and the gloss and finish, wherever it is lacking, will ultimately be polished into being. Always that is a consequent and collateral matter.

Tonight as I write these words there are more plays being done in America than ever before, and that in spite of the war. And there are ten times as many people seeing them as were seeing the Broadway product in those lamented twenty-five years ago. In the last twelve months alone there were more than four hundred thousand, nearly half a million, amateur theatre productions of plays in the United States. At least thirty play-agent firms such as the Dramatists Play-Service, Samuel French, and Walter Baker are engaged full time in handling the rights and royalties for this multitudinous business. Only yesterday one of the big agents told me that the amount of royalties paid in by these non-professional groups for any six of the Broadway successes annually is well up towards a hundred thousand dollars and increasing. So much for finances.

No, the American theatre is not dying, it is alive and flourishing as it never has been. Only the Broadway theatre is dying. Nor is it actually dying, for that matter. It is only being whittled down to its proper place and size in the national scheme of things. And that is good for all concerned, and it will be good when we realize it. The people's theatre is no longer an extension of Broadway. Rather the reverse. Broadway is a part of the people's theatre and only a part. The facts prove that and no more than that. And as Broadway has shrunk on down to the point where its twenty-eight current productions are about equal to its needs and abilities, and as the professional playhouses, the old opera houses and academies of music have disappeared under the onslaught of the movies and machine-made entertainment, just so has this people's theatre proportionately increased.

So far as I know there has not been a single playhouse erected in New York City since the Ziegfeld Theatre was built there on Sixth Avenue and Fifty-fourth Street some twenty years or more ago. But look what has happened in the "provinces." In that time literally thousands have been built—from coast to coast and from the Gulf to the Great Lakes. In the last ten years more than a billion dollars has been spent on theatres and equipment in the non-professional field. And all of them are in use the majority of the nights and days of the year. Here our young people, eager and happy, are working away, shaping, building, creating and giving expression to the abundance of life and joy and the artist's urge that pulses in them.

Again I wish I could call the roll, telling about the countless groups and what they are doing—there in Seattle, at Stanford, in Wisconsin, Minnesota, the Dallas Little Theatre, the University of North Carolina, Loyola, Williams, Penn State, Texas, Iowa, Cornell, Cleveland, Pasadena, Dartmouth, Oberlin, Carnegie Tech, Vassar, Smith, Syracuse, Rollins, Swarthmore, Mount Holyoke, Washington and Lee, Amherst, Stephens, Hunter, down

in Athens and the deep South where poverty and economics are supposed to put out the light, Miami, Shreve-
port, Little Rock, and on up to Indiana with its new million
dollar playhouse—but I have neither the space nor the
time here. That is a thrilling and tremendous story in itself, separate and apart. And what makes it so thrilling
and tremendous is that at last and for the first time in the
history of our country the theatre is finally being recognized as a vitalizing and powerful force in the education,
development, and cultural requirements of our people—
that is, recognized everywhere except on Broadway.

Then let us lift up our discouraged and pessimistic
heads from this same Broadway and look out across the
country and see what is under way and happening, see the
meaning and feel the inspiration of it all. And as we
glimpse the opportunity there, it is inconceivable that we
won't want to share in it, won't want to meet the challenge,
yes, supply the market waiting for our talents and what
these talents can produce. If we do that we shall no longer
have reason to complain that the theatre is dying or dead.

Then who will take the lead among us in service to this
mighty and imaginative enterprise? Let the key men do it.
Let the playwrights act. The rest will follow. Let O'Neill,
Sherwood, Anderson, Kaufman, Barry, Connelly, Saroyan, Behrman, Odets, Hart, Kingsley, and others start
writing directly for this people's theatre without fouling
and choking and stifling their plays further in the consti-
pated and disordered gut of Broadway. Some have already started. Let the others do likewise. And in so doing,
I for one believe we all will again touch upon those springs
of wonder and encouragement which first we knew in
earlier and happier Times Square days.

Of course there will be matters of management of the unions, of contracts and the thousand and odd ends of old selfish and blind economic claimants to dispense with. But it can be done if we love our art and love the welfare of our souls as artists enough. Arrangements can always be made, difficulties can always be ironed away before the compulsion of a passionate spirit. What we need is passion for the job, and if we realize the meaning of the job we shall certainly get the passion and energy to put it through. It is up to us—playwrights, actors, producers, designers, artists all—and up to us now to give our coöperation to this people's theatre in America. Broadway still has a lot to offer. Then let it offer it freely and determinedly, and thus the more surely may it save itself. For only the giver shall keep his power to give. This is an old truth well-known in religion and love. It is the same truth for art also, for the three come into being and fulfillment much the same mysterious way, don't they?

So then as workers all together in a vast and coöperative endeavor we can the more surely hope and expect to see the theatre of our dreams come true. Here in America we have all the material, the passions, the hopes, the ideals, the hates, the antagonisms, the breaking and building of lives, the varying nationalities, the rich backgrounds of folk customs, music, legends, and beliefs out of which to create a native American drama which might well rival the two other proud ages of the world—the Greek and Elizabethan. Our mighty engineers and builders, our politics and our folk heroes, our daily deeds themselves, our boundless and compelling enterprises of wheels and dollars—all likewise cry out the drama that is turmoiling and seething in them. It is up to us to help shape this drama, speak its message and meaning and set it free for the joy and final encouragement of man for which it was meant. To do this all are needed—together. And it cannot be done in a Broadway bottleneck.

A Note on Tragedy

1

UNTIL RECENTLY THERE WERE STILL A FEW NAÏVE and incredulous souls who refused to believe that this country is now involved in one of the greatest crises of its history. Blissful, as it were on flowery beds of ease, they lay dreaming of stocks and bonds and pretty girls to come and waved the bothersome fact away—an elegant hand against a trifling fly that disturbed their rest. And when the nightmare face of the rumored truth even intruded for an instant into their deep and lethargic sleep they turned over, smiled and murmured something about fantasy, idle make-believe and dollies. "Go away, quit playing Halloween," they said.

Then the earth burst open that Sunday morning at Pearl Harbor, and in the midst of flying timbers and shocking reverberations they too were finally loud awake. And instinctively in their irritation, stupefaction, and pain they called out who, why, what, and how? And the voices of democratic authority speaking in the air tentatively told them. And a blank of firm commitment was handed in for them to sign like the rest of us as citizens and soldiers in a raging war.

Today we are all awake and fighting. Only in the cradle (the madhouse, and the grave) are there innocence, ignorance, and neutrality. And the war we now fight is unlike all other wars in its breadth and mounting intensity. From almost any vantage point it is a world civil war, and its destructive reach and violence are engulfing the globe, dividing nation against nation and often the people inside a nation against themselves. All the ancient woes, tribulations, and horrors of an Apollo or angry Jehovah have come upon us multiplied. For the first time in its history mankind is today primarily engaged in killing and being killed. The universal engine and machine have made it possible. Pain, not joy, is our common lot from pole to pole, and pain unlike joy knows no surfeit, never grows familiar and restful, never makes peace with the sufferer or he with it until one of the two has destroyed the other. This is all an old story now, and we are learning it well.

2

When wars come upon a people or when a people go forth into war—and the more desperate the war the truer it is—physical power and physical needs take their usual precedence over all other values and principles. The spiritual must yield to the bodily, the higher to the lower, at least for a while. For wars, no matter what the crying exhortation and credo of faith floating romantically above them is, are first fought by soldiers, by living moving bodies, with three-dimensional instruments, means of destruction as well as protection, offence and defence. And in any fight for survival of one enemy over another it will always be so. For here is no running at tag, no give and take of gaming, no mockery and mummery any longer, no fanciful indulgence of the imagination, no play-acting in a snug and peaceful theatre. This is the bloody drama of life and death in earnest. And here the men that fall with bullets in their hearts are actual corpses and will arise no more from seeming so to walk the boards of life again. All is over and done for with them. The pale film covering their eyes is the veil of eternal death. This is their actual red and salty blood sinking irrevocably into the stage of earth. That is a fire there that consumes the building itself, properties, costumes, and all attendant theatrical trappings of the actor and his pride. Here are actual violence and waste and rot in their complete and active finality. Further into dramatic realism one cannot go. There has been talk and talk about it—in song and story, by the fireside, at the huskings, from the pulpit and studio, in the country store, on the stage, the screen, but this is it, the real thing. This is a game for keeps. This is war.

Yet when anguish and suffering take possession of a people they at the first opportunity the more begin to search and inquire for the principles of life and reality and value behind and beyond the pain and death. So today we do. Collectively and individually we are taking stock of ourselves perhaps as never before. No longer is it a matter of prime capital and physical holdings in dollars and cents and easeful sleep with us but of the more vital and uplifting ideals which feed and energize and

clothe the human spirit. We are asking ourselves in this
tragic hour whether we possess these ideals or not and if so
how much and of what quality, saying if we do not possess
them how can we lay hold of them to salvation. For now
men everywhere are undone, and through what sin or
moral lack in us have we helped to bring the affairs of the
human race to this pass? Like Job we plead the wherefore
and for what reason. And unlike Job, since we live in a
scientific dispensation, we know that no answer will come
to us from a conveniently risen whirlwind. We must find
it in and among ourselves, one with another. And we are
searching for the answer even as we fight, searching the
more zealously, the harder we fight.

3

These first forty-three years of the twentieth century
have been a time of great waste and upheaval as well as
spiritual lethargy in the United States, even as in other
parts of the world. We have fought and finished one world
war, scrambled and argued away the fruits of its victory,
continued our great splurge of building and spending and
production of engineering miracles, created our palaces
of mammon, hawked and gambled and frantically traded
therein, sunk to the bottom of a vicious depression, broken
many of the most sacrosanct and basic axioms of capital-
istic philosophy and free enterprise, torn up and scrapped
in our blinded groping some of our most cherished political precedents and findings of the founding fathers, and
now have embarked stern-faced and purposeful with all
sails set and bands and banners blowing into this grim and
more total business of dying and causing to die. Now the

country is upsurging, boiling over in an aroused frenzy of labor and devotion to the world job to be done. And isolationism is ending, soon to be ended—we say.

Though this ferment and activity and lavish display of overpowering enterprise may not mean a like expansion and growth of ideals they are at least a sign of fierce and healthful life and energy at work. Out of it all something new may develop, even the new face of a transformed world. And we hope something great will be born—a principle of human idealism, a social philosophy and practice which will make the earth a better and more coöperative place in which to live, a great art or literature to help in the liberation and vision of mankind, even as Thomas Jefferson dreamed. In some such dawning faith as this we fight this terrific war along with other nations who are also upsurging and boiling and fermenting and searching for something of the same faith.

And how badly and tragically we need a deep and sustaining faith! During this almost half a century each democratic individual with his sacred prerogatives has had to get hold of his own faith by hook or crook and as best he could, and most often he has got hold of nothing. During this time we have had only one great moral political leader, and we ignorantly denied him. Even today in the midst of our falling egocentric institutions there are some, however loyal and patriotic they be, who hold his teachings of coöperation suspect. And most of the gamblers, big and little, with raking arms around the table stakes still renounce him bitterly. His vision of a federated peaceful world is still obscured by the cigar smoke of the plush chair strategists and maneuvrists and haters of the day. And as for our other prophets and

leaders and spokesmen they have been few and far between and timid and uncertain at that. They have been
unable to speak clearly and authoritatively in the realm of
faith which is the need of our crying, begging souls. But
they have been most voluble and pat about materials,
methods, processes, regulations and directives in the province of things, and machines of force and battle. This looks
like the cart before the horse as any good Hindu, Chinese,
or Hebraist gazing up from his holy book could tell you.
For if faith does not precede action, then how blind and
ruinous the action must be. But whether the horse pulls
the cart or the cart runs away with the horse, for the immediate present the results in destruction and killings are
the same. For we are involved in this war, and we have no
choice but to go headlong through it with all possible speed
and power. The physical and accidental survival demands
of the dilemma compel us to fight now and think later, or
at most think as best we can while the battle thunders,
intending, so help us God, to think clearer and more chari-
tably as soon as the crisis eases a little, and then to act
accordingly. Thus will we do our part in bringing beneficence and healing to a war-torn world.

Yes, man must have a faith or he is utterly undone. The
way of the tooth and animal claw, the red survival of the
fittest, is contrary to his deeper nature as man. Even to
consider it is to know it. He is not an animal. In suffering he again discovers it.

4

For there are never any such self-searchings, queryings,
and contemplations of soul as these among the animals.

There is nothing spiritual in the animal world, no human and promethean foresight, no epimethean hindsight, no looking before or after, no weighing of meaning or results. Only shelter and food, and sex and play, and war and slumber. Nor is there hope or regret there, no aspiration, no pangs and tensions of conscience, no tragic or divided self, no comic completeness. There nothing seems to exist except the process of animal life itself, and by its very nature it is self-continuing. It cannot cease, cannot commit mass suicide. It can only change its form. The sauropoda may die, but the reptile, the lizard process continues. And when and if the species does change, that change happens without the free functioning of its intelligence and will. It comes about through the cryptic and mystic workings of natural law, of an immanescent functioning of physical and material cause and effect. It is a resultant of nature. With man it is otherwise.

When the chipmunk stores up its grain, or the wren makes fat and warm its nest, or the tulip drinks its soothing April rain it does so instinctively and without comprehension of choice. It is a pure fact of the instant, complete and timeless in itself, and is real and significant to the chipmunk, to the wren, to the flower in that instant only, no matter what the unconscious result of that storing up, that making fat and warm, that drinking may be. In the natural world there are only seeing and doing in the eternal simplicity and sensitivity of the moment. Whether one considers nature to be an everlasting succession of such actions and reactions or an endless stream of pre- and unconscious behavior the truth is the same. And though the paleontologist may prove all-inclusively that the earth's crust has been the graveyard of countless forms of bio-

logical existence, showing if need be that more species are
now extinct than are extant and man also will likewise
dolefully perish in this same nature, still we the non-
scientists know that man somehow stands apart and above
this universal burial and condemnation unto death, however precariously he stands. For he knows the fact of such
condemnation and in that knowledge retains something of
superiority to that fact, as the knowing subject over the
object known, no matter what happens to his animal part,
the body.

5

Yes, man is a spirit charged with knowledge and the
responsibility of that knowledge. He lives in a kind of
mortal immortality different from the immortal mortality
of the animal. His kingdom stretches far beyond that of
nature's blind vitality into the radiance of another world.
Call this extension of man's spirit, this separation and
aloofness from the animal, this cleavage between two
kinds of living, a matter of difference in degree only as the
scientists are wont to do, yet the difference is there. We
intuitively know and feel it. From the moment when as a
growing child we pass from our animal and instinctive
babyhood into the miracle of our rational and thinking
humanhood, we live as reasoning and responsible beings,
conscious of our beginnings and our end upon this earth,
conscious of non-existence, of all-encompassing death
about us if you will. And because we are men and so
consider, we the more strive and endow our deeds with the
effort of permanence, of immortality against death's dis-
solution and decay. In the reach of our soul's visioning
we become the rebel against omnivorous, all-devouring

time. Having the power of deliberation, of choice and deciding, no matter how we got it, we work, use, shape, control this time to our purpose, seeking to fill it with eternal and fadeless images and expressions of ourselves. We build institutions, set up monuments of the most lasting material possible, write books, dramas, dream dreams and embody them forth in immortal thoughts, thoughts of immortality.

As a creative spirit man is a pioneer then into new ways and methods of believing, acting, and thinking never allowed for in the blind stress of matter and the seething of nature's laws and commingling forms. He is a maker of new forms, a manipulator of this same recalcitrant matter, a legislator and adjudicator of a new law, and his way is forward out of the grip of the old animal law of death and darkness into a newer one of life and light. Nor does he bother too much with the darkness behind from whence he came, as he the seeker and the seer climbs up that long path however toilfully that leads to manhood's mastery. In the words of the poet he has loved the stars too dearly to be fearful of the night, or to bother with the sheeted ghosts of its despair. In man and man only lies the possibility of endowing the animal nature in himself with the glory nature never had and never thought to have. This it is that sets him apart from all things else whether living or dead.

6

Now men can live like animals if they will, even like clods of earth if they so desire. This is not only true of individuals but of whole masses of people. And being each a soul's worth and full of potential and ideal accomplishments, the larger and more inclusive the mass the more wasteful and degrading such living becomes. But wherever you find man at his best and finest he lives not as an animal but as a man—an immortal soul. And the path waits straight before him, the shining goal forever beckoning bright ahead. Then why does he so often fail to travel in it, to see it? What is the hindrance, the handicap to his attaining his haven and his home, his reaching the rainbow wonder of the soul at journey's end? How account for his too frequent tragic failure in his quest? Why do falling wars come on him when his heart pleads peace?

In his efforts to create and make actual his dreams and noble enterprises man time and time again runs afoul of his fellows who likewise are bent on the same purpose of creating and building—whether on the same level of intent or not. This is his tragedy, the tragedy of man against man, human purpose against human purpose, and not the tragedy of man against nature, for in nature there is no tragedy. Nature is always neutral, neither for nor against, neither malign nor beneficent. She is only available— either to inspiration or frustration or not. But why do men so run afoul of one another? Why this contradiction between them, this head-on collision of climbing souls?

Well, is not man still swaddled and swathed in trailing clouds of ignorance and fear that blind him? Does he not glimpse the light, the true path only dimly, intermittently? He does not see it steadily and clear, does he? So he often mistakes signs and symbols for what they are not, mirages for reality, the meaning of specific things for other and general things. Often the better will appear the worse to him, or the worse the better. A too narrow loyalty may grip him now, a confusion of preachers and leaders frustrate him there. A blinding emotion or upswirling passion, planted and bred from ancient deeds and circumstance, may flood through him in a crisis of decision and scatter his plans to foolishness. So tricky a thing is the heritage that brought him here. Or it may be allegiance to family, or institution, or nation, or convention or custom, compelling his denial of a larger and more universal allegiance, involving him in a binary onesidedness. Ambition may pull against honesty, love against honor, will against authority, pride against humility, even the spirit against the flesh—numberless the hazards and pitfalls that lie along the path of his endeavor, countless the strains and tensions that tend to divide him in himself. And it could not be otherwise for this is the living nature of being a man— organic, growing, developing as separate and distinct from the unquerying and integrated animal. But the endeavor is there, the effort ever to build himself a better and more perfect life continues in spite of all odds against him, and often because of these very odds.

7

This cross-purpose among men, this opposition and contradiction of ideals and principles have been an abiding source of discouragement and fatalism, of laissez faire acceptance and do-nothing attitude among many a philosopher, artist, scientist, and social and political theorist. For out of such collisions these same wars come, and grievous killings and deeds of anathema and destruction, oppressions and ignorant persecutions occur, and the cherished values of all are put on the griddle of jeopardy. We seem to be able to do nothing against them. This finally

beats our spirits down. But then again why? why? we ask
ourselves. Why do we not learn that this is so? Why do
we continue this perverse and recusant wastage of ourselves and all we are? For do not all men alike of whatever creed, calling or circumstance wish to better themselves? Are they not all forever looking to a brighter and
a better tomorrow than today? Do not all men in the large
want the same thing—happiness, self-fulfillment of themselves, service, stable character, a balance of faculties,
and lasting accomplishment for the good of themselves
and their fellows? And yet in their effort to make these
principles of beneficence and good will prevail they come
not to a working together but too often to an impasse one
with another where no solution of their differences seems
possible, no arbitration, no mutual acceptance of differ-
ing contentions can be had. Neither will or can yield. And
then it is, if the cause is vital, fiery, and bitter enough,
that the strangling hand is reached for the helpless throat,
the tragedy of power and force unleashed, and the ritual
of death's enthronement finds its cult. And all because the
means and methods are mistaken for the purpose and the
end, is it not? Each side wants its values in its own terms.
And to the onlooker it's obvious that the terms must be
mutual. How easy to say but, Lord, how hard to comprehend.

8

Any two inimical points of view or values may both be
good in themselves. In fact they are more often good than
not, or they would never lead man to so fateful a collision
and struggle with his kind. He would not risk all that he
is and hopes to be, even to his life itself, if it were other-

wise. He will die a martyr only to what he feels is best. Physical trappings and baubles of commerce and exploitation are given the go-by in the testing hour in spite of what Marx says, and honor and love and faith and universal principles are finally invoked and defended instead. These are man's best. Then why is it that this best is so often at variance with itself, so ethically divided as it were? The answer is, it is not divided. Man himself has in his partial view of the truth concerned made the division. And because of this partial comprehension, and because he must so consecrate himself to the truth as he sees it, he substitutes the part for the whole, his personal part for the impersonal whole, and in so doing denies to his antagonist the rightness of any other claim, an antagonist who likewise demands his partial view as the truth and the whole truth so help him God. Thus when the issue is drawn in terms of groups or nations, more often than not a resort is had to mass violence and the difference must be settled on the battlefield.

And if history and records stored up for himself by man against ruthless time teach anything, they teach to this same man the folly of such a method of settlement. On the contrary they show that once man embarks on the animal course of tooth and claw not only is his principle's efficacy likely to perish but he himself the champion of it to be choked and shamed in death. The flowers of truth, goodness, and beauty never flourish in the murk of the battlefield. And when the champion of a cause dies in no-man's land (how rightly named!), the cause itself is that much nearer death, and doubly near when both the champion and his adversary die. For both are champions of the truth, whatever the variance in uniforms, language, cus-

toms, or tokens of nationality may be. Each has his different version of the truth, and there the trouble is, there the
reason for these same tokens and emblems and signs of
difference by which each enemy can recognize his foe. And
the more excessive he makes his demands for the part truth
he represents the farther he moves from the whole truth.
In short, the first step made in the direction of violence to
support a principle not only is a denial of the reality which
that principle represents but is a denial of man himself.
He has turned toward animalhood again.

9

Today we are engaged in this world civil war, a battle
between brothers. For as seekers after the truth we are
brothers, brothers invoking identical shibboleths of secu-
rity, health, responsibility, privilege, purpose, happiness
—and calling upon the same God and divine spirit to
bring them to pass. As one family we want a better world
and a better life for ourselves and for all men. The quarrel
has resulted from a difference of view as to how to secure
these blessings. And the attendant circumstances of power,
plunder, and profit have nothing to do with the real reason
for the fight. They are only accidental, the occasion, not
the cause. The democracies declare for liberty of the individual conscience and person, for self-choice and the
moral responsibility of the individual soul, first to itself
and second in actual fact to its neighbor. The enemy of the
democracies believes in the liberty of the state first, the
power of the state over the individuals that make it up,
denying to the individual any prerogatives to himself except the dutiful privilege of serving the state. The state has

total power. There are no such entities as natural rights, and the action of the individual has ultimate meaning only in the action of the group, the state. Only in this way can those blessings and benefits desired by the individual be guaranteed. Left to themselves men will forever compete and rot and degrade one another in a senseless competition, in what the democracies love to call free enterprise, the enemy says. The strong will devour the weak, the weak will hate the strong, and wastage and general degradation of living will result. The democracies challenge this to the death. The one way to degrade man, they say, is to take away his individuality as a man. Rob him of his self-sufficiency, his personal and unique importance, his integrity as a moral self-judging, self-activating soul, that is, absorb his individuality into the society of which he should be a distinctive part, and he is ruined and undone as a man. He has become standardized, mechanized, and dulled beyond regeneration. He cannot think and act for himself.

So the two views are extremes and as such oppose each other today. As partial truths they are antagonistic, each a part of the larger truth—the truth of institutionalized man. James Madison, Benjamin Franklin, Thomas Jefferson, the Adamses, and George Washington said there are certain rights and liberties belonging to man prior to all other rights and duties—rights irrespective of nationality, race, creed, color, or previous condition of servitude, such as life, liberty, and the pursuit of happiness. And a state is an institution created to protect him in these rights, and created only by the consent of the governed for this purpose. The state then is a product of the citizenry and not the citizenry a product of the state. And this being so, then it is the right of the citizenry at any time to remake the state when it ceases to function as its servant. For only a government based upon a recognition of these principles has a right to be, only so can it function freely and survive.

Again the opponents of this view are just as certain of the truth they hold. So was Alexander Hamilton certain, many a thoughtful Tory in the old days like Governor Hutchinson of Massachusetts, so are Hitler, Mussolini, and Tojo today. To them the state was and is in the last analysis the all. A government is only a government worth the name when it is strong and centralized—a government to which men owe undying and absolute obedience and which exercises its right over them either by divine authority from heaven, or the commandment of race, or the stern and unyielding law of biology.

Now neither of these is separately and wholly true. For the citizen makes the state and the state makes the citizen. Each lives in its relationship to the other. This is the reality and meaning of both. And neither can exist apart from the other either in sequence of time or logic. It is true by definition. And yet prior to them all and abiding there when their reaches and realm are ended is man himself, the living soul, single with himself, alone with his deliberation and intent. In giving recognition to this fact it would seem that democracy as a system has at last made a beginning in the problem of government among men, no matter what its abuses have been.

Whatever the method by which the adherents to the opposing views have come to their belief, their summons to the field, their battle cries and exhortations to victory, I say, are identical, which proves my point—"God helping us we can do no other," they both cry. "The destiny of our people is at stake," "This is an historic hour, a thousand years of history look down on you," "Our cause is just and we shall prevail," "Choose now whether it shall be chains and slavery or a hero's grave," "As for us give us liberty or give us death," "We are fighting for the freedom of the world," "My country right or wrong," "*Deutschland über alles*,"—And so it goes. And the more high-sounding and idealistic the principles of individualism or nationalism called upon, the more deadly the battles resulting in their name. And there is no solution or stopping the tragedy and the flow of blood until one side or the other has yielded. But then in this yielding there is no remedying of the trouble. The defeated one is not converted, only beaten. And all the shouting and the flags and flowers, the bouquets thrown, the speeches made, the bright smiles and welcomes, the kisses and parades cannot hide away the horror of waste and death that lies around. And this woe and pain had better never been. "Yes, we fought a good fight," says the winning side, "and God has crowned our arms with victory." "Yes, we fought a good fight," says the loser, "and on a day we'll fight again. Then, God helping us, it will be different."

Both sides were right, and only partly right. In the excess and exclusiveness of their claims they both were wrong. The totalitarian point of view has a truth, the truth of social responsibility. The individualistic point of view has a truth, the truth of freedom. Separate they clash, together they make more of a whole, but not even here the final whole, for that finality lies in the fact of a totality of individuals and nations coöperating as members of the human race. Then the privileges of the part become the responsibilities of the whole and there is no place for rabid nationalism or personal license left. A man's duty to

himself and state is his duty to the world, and his duty to
the world is his duty to himself and state. Every right has
here a corresponding responsibility, and vice versa every
freedom a corresponding duty, and likewise every duty a
privilege. And for each there is a time, a place and a right
and fittingly peaceful method of bringing it to action. And
the problem is to find out how this can be done, peacefully
and thoughtfully and never by resort to wild and ungov-
ernable arms.

10

Now what has this to do with the art of tragedy—dramatic tragedy, the kind the playwrights write?

Everything. For these conflicts, tensions, efforts, oppo-
sitions and struggles are the source of tragedy. From this
dualism of facts and battling theories the artist can shape
his story and write his drama. In reality here and here
only will he find the story and drama worthy of his effort
—whether it be comic or whether it be tragic. And likewise only in so using his talents and creative powers does
he become worthy of what he tries to shape and embody
forth. Let the artist then think on this, brood on it, understand this process of things and way of man's endeavor,
comprehend the direful depths of its meaning and so set
forth in the bright illumination of his art the nobler and
more inclusive truth of their reason and their right, their
excesses and their wrongs. In the synthesis of his conclusion the higher value will stand revealed. And as it stands
revealed to man's gaze so will it demand and get the loyalty and devotion of the gazer—all men alike.

Here rests the challenge and the duty of the artist. Here
the reason for his being what he is. And in this effort and

this alone can he become fulfilled as an artist, can his art speak its universal message of coöperation and joy, of life and not death, of inspiration not failure, of beauty not ugliness. And in this then he becomes once more the rightful prophet and his message a religious and uplifting one as from the first it was meant to be.

11

And there was Athens on a hill—the city beautiful, the joy of the world and sunrise hymns in olden days. Neither floods nor fire nor earthquake nor anger of the gods destroyed her. But she is dead—gone, trampled and hammered into dust by the impious feet of marching ignorant men.

And the roll-call of blasted hopes and beauty broken runs malignly on through the centuries and in wider lands to little Gela where sleep the bones of mighty Aeschylus, shamed in the tragic tramp of the lonely doughboy going by—Aeschylus father of our drama whom the long-haired Mede knew well and the Athenian loved—and on to Naples now and Rome and Turin and the glory that is Milan, caught and ground and shattered in the cracking-jawed compress of all-powerful and brutish war.

"O Sophocles, son of Sophillus, singer of choral odes, Attic star of the tragic muse, whose locks the curving ivy of Acharnae often crowned—a tomb and a little portion of earth hold thee, but thy exquisite life shines yet in thy immortal page!"

That is the one cause, that is the higher truth—the immortal page. Let us create and seek to save it!

For that we fight—even to contradiction.

Evening Sun Go Down

MY OLD FRIEND THE MILLER HAS DEFINITE IDEAS on a lot of subjects including the Southern Negro. Recently I was sitting with him in his mill-house, as I often do, helping him shell his yellow corn when he turned to me and said, "What is the biggest mistake this country ever made?"

I thought awhile and then said I didn't know, unless it was the Civil War. That had seemed to me a useless and tragic thing.

"No doubt about that being a mistake, all right," he said, "with its killings and destruction, but it weren't the biggest by a long shot."

"No?"

"No. For the biggest was the bringing of the Negro to our shores. Look about you. Everywhere you turn we are reminded of it. Just before you drove up in your car, Fannie Privett and her seven mulatto young'uns come

149

dragging by begging for a peck of meal. I gave it to her, and she went on down the road to her cabin, with her kids plundering and proguing in the edge of the woods hunting for bullaces, 'simmons, pinemast, and anything else they could pick up. And there's not only one family like that in this neighborhood but several. And from Texas to Baltimore you will find them like that—traipsing, drabble-tailed people living on the scum and picking the garbage of the world. Oh, yes, the orators and you writers and teachers keep preaching and talking a lot about what a great thing freedom has been for the Negro race. I wonder. The truth is, they're not free. And we the white men are not free either. They pull us down on every hand, and as we pretend to try to pull them up."

"But we don't pretend," I replied. "We actually do. Look at the school buildings we're putting up for them—the education, the better health."

"What education, what better health?" he asked irritably, and then went on. "Take my Tom mule. I keep him fat, curry him, look after him, and he does my work, and he helps produce his own feed besides. Suppose I said to him, 'Tom, I'm Abraham Lincoln, in this year of our Lord 1862, and I'm going to set you free. No more gall of trace chains and sweating in the summer fields. No.' So I open the stable door and lot gate and say, 'Get out. You're a free mule. You're on your own, and root hog or die.' And out goes Tom kicking up his heels, feeling free and happy as a lark, jolly as a doodle bug. But what happens to Tom? He winds up like the Negro—yeh—hard up, down in the dry reed swamp or in a briar patch. And if he's got any sense he'll be back at my lot gate soon braying for me to take him in, ready to get back into the harness and do what

I tell him. Yes, we say we've freed the Negro. And what has he got out of it? I'll tell you—his one gallus, his plough-handle, his digging at the bottom, his poor wages, flies and hovels, dysentery and disease. That's the sort of thing he's got. Go up there in town and talk to Dr. Rainer. He'll tell you. Let him show you his files."

"I know there's that side to it," I said, "but that's not all. You forget their music, the work of certain individuals like Carver, like—"

"It's enough," he jeered. "What I'm getting at is this— if we're going to free him, let's do it. Do you know what the average pay for Negro cooks is in this neighborhood?"

"No, I don't."

"Well, being as you're always writing about the Negro you ought to look into it. It runs from five to six dollars a week—and I mean a week of fifty-five or sixty hours too —with an old hand-out dress now and then or a mouldy hambone thrown in. Now is any mother of a household, black or white, that works for such a wage free and self-respecting? I ask you."

"Well, it's pretty poor wages, that's true. But the people aren't able to pay more."

"Who said they weren't able to pay more?"

"They do—the people."

"If they'd all get together and decide to pay more, they could."

"But how are they going to get together? Our economy is geared to—"

"That's just it—let them decide to do it and stick to it— fight on back up the line to their own wages above. If they spent as much time really trying to coöperate on such things in this country as they do talking about individualism, and freedom and the American way of life, they'd get somewhere. Take all these speeches of Henry Wallace —no, I won't go into that. I tell you when this war and world of evil has faded from the battlefields, this country's got to do something about revising its Declaration of Independence and its Constitution—especially its Constitution, since I reckon it's too late to change the Declaration. We've got to do something about capital and labor, set forth the place and meaning of each, and we've got to do something about this Negro business."

"That's exactly what Mr. Wallace says."

"But we've got to apply commonsense to it and not the dole or some W. P. A. idea that he and the president talk about. You can't subsidize people into being good citizens and self-reliant souls that way. The only way is for them to earn what they deserve and what they get—give 'em a chance to earn it. Yessir, the poor old South is cursed from Sodom to Gomorrah—by the Negro and our mishandling of him. Just suppose we didn't have any Negroes among us—what a different people we'd be!—stronger, better brains, characters, better everything. They're ruining us and we're ruining them. We keep them in the ditch, the briar patch and the swamp, and in keeping them there we have to stay with them."

"What would you do—send them back to Africa?"

"Of course you can't send them back to Africa. They're here with us—citizens, such as they are, with their rights, privileges, and responsibilities. Don't forget that—responsibilities. So I say if we're going to meet the problem we've got to do it in a wholehearted, commonsense manner. We've got to use authority over them, the way I do over

Tom. We've got to be clear-headed and hard. Yes, you heard me—hard as well as fair."

"That sounds a little like Fascism or Nazism, doesn't it?"

"I don't care what it sounds like," he answered abruptly, "just so it makes sense. There's no sense in the way we're running things now. You know that. You spoke of education and schools. Look what we do there. We put up two school buildings where we ought to put up only one. Why? Because one has to be for the black man and his sun-burnt relatives and another has to be for the white man. Why? Is there a white education and a black education? Is knowledge a matter of color? Our glorious old commonwealth seems to think so, for a colored woman can hold an A certificate and a white woman the same certificate, and the state says the white woman's is worth more than the colored's, and the pay check is made out accordingly. Seems to me Jefferson and the founding fathers talked a lot about equal abilities having a chance at equal rewards. If the American way of life that everybody beats their gums about in this global war don't mean that, what does it mean? No, sir, we act just like, say, there was a Negro multiplication table and a white folks' table, and like two times two is four for some people and three and a half for others. Does that make sense? For instance, if we build a bus station we've got to go to the expense of building two waiting rooms, white and colored. Every filling station has to have its four separate restrooms —for white men and white women, for Negro men and Negro women. No wonder they all stay so dirty. It's too expensive to keep 'em clean. And every railroad station has its separate places for the Negro and the white man to

stand and look at each other through the bars, breeding
suspicion and night-time trouble. There's no sense in that.
It don't add up to the truth."

"Then you mean the solution is race equality?"

"That's the question they always raise up—the old
question of race equality, and whether I'd want my daughter to marry a black man. Equality depends on the character of the individuals concerned and is not a matter of
laws and iron bars. That's the way I see it. And as for the
marrying matter, I ain't got a daughter. If I did have, I'd
say let her take care of that when it came up. The thing to
deal with is what's before us now—the mess and waste
and degeneration we've got into. And to do that we've got
to be honest, got to get up manhood enough to face this
thing, wipe out these barriers and double dealings, put the
Negro on his own, give him a chance to be a man as he
wants to be, a chance to earn a decent living, raise his
wages, let him in the labor unions, give him a chance in
politics, a vote, a say-so in public affairs, let him become
a real citizen with a country he belongs to and one that
belongs to him. And he'll rise up to meet his opportunity
then. He'll become somebody, sure as shooting. That's the
way humanity behaves and always will no matter what
the place, the color, the creed, or previous condition of
servitude. And if we do that, then I won't have the insult
of such old hussies as this one that's just been here coming
up to me and saying and begging in a whining voice,
'Please suh, gimme a little meal for me and my poor
chillun—gimme suh!' If that means race equality, then
I'm for it. Yes, sir, this country's made a lot of mistakes.
It was a mistake to fight the war of 1812. The Civil War
was a grievous mistake. Going over there into Asia and

putting our fingers in the Philippine pie and our head in
the kindly open door of China was a mistake. We oughta
got it hung in the crack, and by golly sometimes it looks
like we did. The Monroe Doctrine was a mistake, narrow-
minded and one-sided, saying 'you can't play in my front
yard but I'm going to play in yours.' Yessir. But the greatest mistake of all was when our forefathers brought the
Negroes to this country. Now let's get busy and wipe out
this mistake."

"I agree with you. We ought to do it—"

"Yes, I know you do," he replied, "from the books you
write I'd know that. But you're like too many of the folks
down here—too talky, easy, and wishy-washy. You've got
to quit talking and go to work on the problem—be hard,
put your foot down, be scientific about it, as they say up at
your university. Yessir, use authority and the strong hand,
discipline, cut out this soft paternal Santa Claus stuff."

"You're right," I said.

"You're dang right I'm right," he said.

A wagon turned in from the highway and came knocking across the mill yard toward us. The old man looked
out through the open door and held his ear of corn still for
a moment in his hand. I followed his gaze and saw a bent-
over young Negro man sitting on the wagon seat draped
in an old shawl and pulled along by a poor shaky and raw-
bony mule.

"There you are again," said the miller gesturing with
the ear of corn and then beginning to shell it rapidly with
the butt of his palm. "That's Claude Young bringing his
corn to be ground. He's half-paralyzed from a bad blood
disease. Some low-down woman has hamstrung him and
burnt his life away. Every time I see him his tongue's a

little stiffer and his words harder to understand. Now ain't that a fix for a young fellow to get into? No telling how many colored girls he's contaminated too."

"Yes, it's bad," I said dolefully.

"Somebody ought to put the law on him and make him get cured up," said the miller.

"I sent him to Dr. Rainer once myself," I said, "but he didn't go back."

"Hah, there you are!" the old man exclaimed, throwing out his hands testily.

The wagon drew up in front of the door, and the Negro made a blubbering heigh-oing noise in his throat.

"Wait a minute, son," the old miller called out suddenly and kindly, "we'll help you with that heavy sack!"

The two of us went out and lifted down the bag from the wagon. And the Negro Claude sat aloft and silent in his seat, his face cryptic, tragic, and expressionless.

"How're you feeling, Claude?" I asked.

"Po'ly, Mitha Paul," he managed to answer, still staring lightlessly before him.

Beyond the rim of pines that skirted the millpond to the west the autumn sun was going down in a splurge of violent color, dyeing the world and sky high and wide with its flame. Like a great fiery eye it was going down, and for an instant it seemed to peer out at me with a mocking jaundiced gleam.

"We'll have your meal in a jiffy, Claude," the old miller called cheerily. And Claude sat bent like a crooked stump under his ragged shawl, saying nothing, saying nothing at all as we two Southern theorists got busy serving him.

And while I watched his corn a-grinding, a lump kept

rising in my throat, the lump that rises in the throat of
the soft indulgent South. (God help my land or anywhere
when the steel of machinery and cold statistics takes that
lump away!) And I grieved over his crippled and spoiled
young life, seeing him so quiet and waiting there, so
lonely and so humble there under the great down-bending
sky. Nothing but sympathy and love could I feel for him,
and neither blame nor anger at all for any of his sins
and wild misdoings.

Then we carried his meal back out to him.

"Claude," I finally said.

"Etha, Mitha Paul," he gulped in answer.

"You'll have to go with me up to see Dr. Rainer again
tomorrow."

"Etha, Mitha Paul," he mumbled meekly.

He understood and I understood—he my suffering
care for him and I his gentle meekness. And because it
was so I felt a little glad, and I knew he was glad. And
the final wink of the wise all-seeing sun was not so mocking any longer now, as the huge thumb of the tree-dark
hill extinguished it. And I was glad too to remember suddenly that I had forgot all about authority and the case
of stern redeeming law, for the moment I had.

The boy dragged on his rope reins, stirred a bit pain-
fully in his seat, and drove slowly and knockingly away.

"We'll work these things out down here somehow," I
said, half into the air and half to distant human ears—
"somehow we will."

"I hope so," said the old miller resignedly.

And standing there silent we watched the ramshackle
wagon fade away in the sweet enfolding gloom.